A Bristol Panorama

Doreen Street

REDCLIFFE
Bristol

First published in 1992 by
Redcliffe Press Ltd
49 Park St, Bristol.

© Doreen Street

ISBN 1 872971 62 8

British Cataloguing-in-Publication Data.
A catalogue record for this book is available
from the British Library.

Typeset and printed by
The Longdunn Press Ltd., Bristol.

Contents

Credits

The Samuel Loxton drawings on pages 9, 20, 40, 43 and 52 were reproduced by courtesy of the Bristol Reference Library, College Green, Bristol.

Mary Robinson by Gainsborough on page 55 was reproduced by courtesy of The Trustees of the Wallace Collection, London.

The Blue Bowl Inn reproduced on page 36 by kind permission of David Elliot.

Sarah Ann Henley on page 71 by courtesy of the Reece Winstone collection.

One

Kingswood 1928–38 – King John's Lodge – Kingswood Castle

Kingswood 1928–38

Many older residents of Kingswood have fond memories of childhood visits to the old Regent Cinema. Too young to appreciate the tragic charm of Gloria Swanson or Mary Pickford, they would have chuckled at the antics of a silent Charlie Chaplin.

On Saturdays in those happily unsophisticated times, there was usually a pavement artist who drew his pictures on paving slabs near Zion Chapel. He gave young children their first introduction to the art world. Then there was a woman who had a gramophone mounted on a baby's pram. Through its brightly painted trumpet came the sound from scratchy records which were played over and over again in an effort to earn a few coppers.

A popular shop was Swaish's which boldly displayed the pawn-shop trade sign of three balls, jokingly said to imply 'two to one you won't get back what you have pawned'.

There were several of these shops around the Bristol area owned by Alderman Sir John Swaish who lived near Willsbridge Hill.

A local story tells how, in the old days, when on his way to business Sir John could frequently be seen sat alongside the driver of a lorry owned by a market gardener. Sir John wore his morning coat and silk top hat, and the spuds and cabbages were piled up behind him.

His son George Swaish R.A. painted a life-size portrait of his father as Lord Mayor of Bristol, which was presented to the City Art Gallery.

I remember those lovely cream slices and iced buns which the bakery shops sold for one penny each, or seven for sixpence ($2\frac{1}{2}$p). At Easter time the bakery shop used to pay boys commission for getting orders for hot cross buns and delivering them. One crafty individual to whom I had never spoken, attempted to blackmail my mother into placing her order with him. "Your Dorrie is my young lady," he lied. "If you don't give me an order I shall pack her up."

One of the most disliked institutions at Kingswood was the Labour Exchange. In the years of the 'Depression' which followed the great Wall Street crash, hundreds of men queued up daily to sign on for the weekly 'dole' money. They stood waiting in all winds and weathers, sometimes for hours. Many were wearing threadbare clothes and worn out shoes. I believe that the unemployment benefit at that time was 27 shillings (135p) per week for a man and his wife and two shillings for the eldest child and one shilling each for any other children.

After drawing the dole money for a few weeks then came the degrading 'Means Test'. If the presiding committee of this inquisition gave a man the 'thumbs down' there was nothing else to do but beg, borrow, or steal. A neighbour of ours attended one of these interviews. His dole money was stopped and he was told, "Let your father keep you." The father was an old age pensioner with no other income but his ten shillings per week pension (50p).

Most shopping centres had their own parade ground, this being a stretch of pavement adopted by teenagers of the district, where in the evenings they went to 'see and be seen', to walk to and fro, or stop to talk. If the weather was inclement they crowded into shop doorways, soon to be moved on by the local policeman. Kingswood's parade reached from South Road to the Clock Tower, and as the girls passed by the lads would whistle Laurel and Hardy's signature tune.

Each parade had its well-known characters. Kingswood had its Billy Flat-a, who was never seen without his cap which he wore perched flat on his head. He walked up and down the High Street carrying a basket with a lid. When asked what was in it, he just smiled and tapped the side of his nose with his index finger.

No girl would be seen talking to Billy, until one day for a dare, a certain young lady caught hold of his arm and accompanied him for a few yards, then she quickly flicked up the lid of the basket. The boys and girls crowded around – it was half full of dead meatflies. So he then became known as Billy Meatfly.

When Kingswood Park was first opened, the Council put on all sorts of shows. I particularly remember the Beauty Contest, held in the open, to be judged by audience applause. A bevy of local beauties stepped on to the stage one by one; it was obvious that the local hairdresser had been busy doing permanent waves, shampoos and sets. The local lads made remarks like, "I won't be clapping for her, we had a date last week and she let me down." "Don't clap for her, she ain't natural, peroxides her hair she do, my sister said."

Then a contestant who appeared to be rather older than the others stepped on to the stage, wearing a hat which almost hid her face. We assumed she couldn't afford a hair-do like the others.

There were whispers among the older element of the audience such as, "What a nerve she's got, standing up there with those young girls." "Let's clap her for a lark, and take the other show-offs down a peg" said someone in the younger set.

The contestants stepped forward in turn to receive acclamation but the teenagers remained silent.

The lady with the hat stepped forward. We yelled, applauded and shouted our approval for so long, that the rest of the audience gave up and joined in with us.

The lady with the hat was awarded first prize – a crisp pound note.

King John's Lodge

The last time I saw the old house, standing solid and familiar amidst the trees, was on a warm summer evening on June 16th, 1936. Three days later it was just a heap of rubble, having fallen victim to a demolition gang.

The house had stood on the summit of Lodge Hill, Kingswood for centuries. Tradition had it that it was originally built for King John and used when he hunted in the Kingswood Forest. It was marked on ancient maps as 'The Kingswood Lodge', but many knew it as King John's Lodge.

There are reasons to believe that the house was built with rather more in mind than that of a mere hunting lodge, for it was situated on the highest point in Bristol, and commanded panoramic views of the surrounding countryside, and on a clear day the Cotswolds, the Mendips, the Welsh Hills and the Bristol Channel. This well-known vantage point would have played its part during England's troubled times by burning a beacon in the event of invasion. Ironically, during the Second World War, it was noticed that from time to time German

7

Bombers used Lodge Hill and Cossham Hospital to obtain their bearings, and often changed direction at this point.

King John's Lodge and the area surrounding it, was reputed to be haunted. The first houses built on the hill remained empty and it has been said that the first couple of tenants were actually paid to live in them in order to attract tenants for the others.

Ghost stories however did not bother us youngsters, we invented new ones for ourselves, such as the Ghost of Handel Cossham, who could be seen riding a white horse around the nearby Hospital.

The old house had a strange fascination for us. We would often spend our pennies on apples which were sold at the kitchen door. It wasn't that their flavour was anything special, but we could look through the ancient doorway to see the ingle-nook fireplace with its roasting spits, and see the grey flagstoned passage.

On the west side of the house were some ruins which we thought must have been a tower where fair maidens had languished as they awaited their Sir Launcelots.

As we walked away counting our apples we got the greatest thrill of all when we peered through a grating in the path that surrounded the house into a dark cavity. Somehow we knew that this must be the 'dungeons' where hapless prisoners had been tortured and in whispers we spoke of the skeleton who walked at night rattling his chains.

It was also common knowledge that there was a secret tunnel in the vicinity but no one had ever seen it.

The Lodge was once used as the headquarters of the Forest Warden and the forest keepers. Later it housed the Duke of Beaufort's stewards, who managed the Duke's coal-mines.

There is a story that a steward who had been drinking heavily jovially challenged His Grace to a fight but the Duke, who was sober, was not amused and the steward was slung out of the Lodge.

My father told me that during the coal-strike in the 1920s, a small number of men dug into the hill near the Lodge and when only a few feet down they struck a seam of coal. From the yield of this miniature coal-mine they were able to make a few shillings for themselves. One man either possessing a strong sense of humour or a poor spelling ability erected a sign which read 'Minator Mine'.

Several years later when the innocence of childhood was outgrown, I was able to look over the Lodge and through the west window, on the top floor of its three storeys, I saw the River Severn

Kingswood Lodge

Kingswood Lodge by Samuel Loxton.
Above: Facing north.
Below: The west side of the lodge.

shining in the sunlight like a silver ribbon.

Later I was to learn that in 1615 the surveyor, John Norden, describing the Kingswood Forest said,

> As for Lodges there is not one in use now. One there was of great antiquity knowne by the name of The Olde Lodge – A second was built by, and in the time of King Henry VIII. The use whereof altered and converted to an ale house standing in the principle part of the forest on the hill fittest for the Lodge to keepe deere, now fit to harbor thieves and enemies of the deere.

The Lodge was demolished in 1936, and after the walls came down, and the rubble was being removed I went to view the foundations with a couple of my former playmates to ascertain if the legends of our childhood had any substance, and if King John could possibly have sojourned here.

Excitement began as just below ground level massive stone-work appeared, the foundations of a bastion tower, and a fortification dating to King John's time. Two vaults were uncovered and lay open to the sky – these were our dungeons, the largest measuring about 18ft by 10ft. More exciting still – on its east side was a doorway, beyond which was the entrance to the long-lost subterranean passage, flanked on each side by roughly hewn rock. It was running in an easterly direction and possibly led to the site of the former Kingswood Castle, which had stood at Soundwell about a quarter of a mile away.

This was just another of the many underground tunnels found in the area once known as the Kingswood Forest.

Kingswood Castle

In the summer of 1968 digging operations on Bristol Waterworks property at Soundwell, Kingswood, revealed the base of a round tower and traces of furnaces which long ago burned coal from the Kingswood Forest.

Until the 1920s the old tower could be seen standing on this site. In Victorian times it was castellated and incorporated into a house, by a Mr Cramer, and was known as 'Kingswood Castle'.

Iron, coal, and the demands of warfare first put this tower on the map in the days of the Civil War.

Oliver Cromwell was familiar with this part of the country having stayed in several of the local houses during his campaigning. One of these was Syston Court, where he left a pair of boots, which were auctioned in 1931 and fetched 13 guineas. He was obviously not bothered about his boots, but he was very concerned about the shortage of iron, essential to the equipment of his forces.

He granted a patent to Captain Copley, one of his officers, to smelt iron by coal in this area where coal was in plentiful supply. But Captain Copley's efforts got off to a bad start. It was said that "he failed to make his bellows blow", so he asked help from Dud Dudley, who had fought as a Cavalier, and is believed to have been hiding out in this area after escaping from Cromwell's forces.

Dud Dudley had experience of coal smelting on the estates of his father Lord Dudley. In his book *Metallum Martis* he gives an account of how he had been taken from his studies at Balliol College to manage his father's furnaces and forges at Dudley. He had discovered that within ten miles of Dudley Castle, 2,000 smiths of all kinds were more or less unemployed and many works were decaying for want of wood. The woods there, as in the Kingswood Forest, were fast disappearing as the trees had been hewn to provide charcoal, which was used until the seventeenth century for iron-smelting.

Coal, however, was in abundance and easily accessible and Dudley's father had obtained a patent for him from King James I for smelting iron from pit-coal.

At first Dudley prospered, but then fell into difficulties as iron-masters of the Worcester area, jealous of his new process, attacked and destroyed his works.

Then came the Civil War and Dudley joined the Cavaliers, fighting with distinction in Sir Francis Worsley's Regiment.

Dudley was taken prisoner at the seige of Gloucester, brought to London and imprisoned. Although wounded he managed, with his typical ingenuity, to escape to Bristol on crutches.

It is fairly certain that Captain Copley built the tower at Soundwell and that in all probability it was a windmill powering the machinery which kept up a continuous current of air in the blast furnaces.

It is not clear what happened to Copley, but Dudley seems to have

11

had trouble with the Bristol and Forest of Dean iron-masters, and he died in poverty. His iron-smelting process was said to have died with him, and was not reintroduced until Abraham Darby set up his works at Coalbrookdale, Shropshire in the eighteenth century.

Kingswood Castle.

Two

Coal miners

Coal-mining was once one of the most important industries carried on around the Bristol area, and up until 1936, miners could be seen on the outskirts of the city coming home from work at the end of the shift, the whites of their eyes gleaming out from their coal-grimed faces. They usually walked in groups with the crunching sound of their hob-nailed boots gradually lessening as one by one they each broke away to turn off at their garden gate.

In those days miners didn't wear pit helmets and didn't have the luxury of pithead baths (how they envied miners of Pensford Colliery which had these installed in 1932).

I remember Grandad coming home from his shift. As he walked down the garden path Grandma took his dinner from the oven, and with a quick wash of his hands, he sat down at the table, knife and fork at the ready, poised for action, and made his usual comment, "Let me get at it, as long as it's not liver."

One day I ventured to ask him why he didn't wash all over before eating. "Read your Bible child," he said between mouthfuls. "That bit about the girl that died, and how Jesus brought her back to life, did he say the first thing to do was to have a wash? Of course he didn't. Told her mother to give her something to eat. So us miners eat as soon as we can after coming up out of the nether regions."

After having mopped his dinner plate clean with a chunk of bread, Grandad would then light his pipe and lean back in his armchair, while Gran was in the kitchen filling the galvanised tin bath with hot water heated in buckets on the gas stove.

When Grandad took his bath Gran was usually in attendance, and he could often be heard to say, "Don't scrub my back so hard Emma, too much water weakens the back."

Miners could often be seen bearing the marks of their calling on various parts of their bodies. Wounds received when working would often heal over with coal-dust still in them and this appeared through the white scars as a dark blue colour.

After bathing and a change of clothes, Grandad could often be found in the pigeon loft (pigeons being the hobby of many miners).

"Wise old birds," he would say. "Can find their way home from anywhere."

Grandpa, too, was a wise old bird. At nightschool he had studied for his Mining Engineer's and Colliery Management certificates and he was also well-versed in the history of coal-mining. On his retirement some found his reminiscences rather boring, but I never did.

History would have us believe that our local colliers in the past were rough and unruly, and in the eighteenth century they were said to be ignorant and heathen; ignorant maybe, but surely not heathen, as even in those days they observed an item of the ancient mining code, dating back to the time of King Edward IV.

That if any man . . . doe by misfortune take his death as by falling ye earth upon him by drowning, stifling by fire or otherwise . . . the workmen of this occupation are bound to fetch ye body out of ye Earth and bring him to Christian burial. Although he be three-score fathoms under the Earth.

Working underground was a dangerous occupation presenting many hazards such as rock falls or water breaking in and flooding the workings. When carbon dioxide mixed with nitrogen it caused suffocation, and methane gas coming in contact with a naked flame caused explosion. At Easton colliery in 1886 methane gas killed five men and endangered the lives of 250. Dr W.G. Grace was quickly on hand to give help to the injured.

Coal miners working underground at the turn of the century.

14

In the old days a great deal of trouble was caused by 'coal-pirates' who, in order to extend the area of their own coal-mines, trespassed into the boundaries of neighbouring pits.

My Grandad never missed the opportunity to point out the 'Warwick Arms' on Charlton Road, Kingswood, as the site of the old Kingswood Lodge pit where in 1833 five boys were trapped for six nights and days without food. Fortunately they were rescued. But six years later, through the avarice of 'coal-pirates' water broke into this pit causing its final flooding and the death of 11 men.

Cossham Hospital was originally built to receive miners and their families. The first four patients were said to have been miners injured in an explosion at Hanham Colliery, two died and two recovered.

Over the centuries miners had developed their own mythology concerning the portends of bad luck; it was especially bad luck to go down into a mine on Good Friday, far better to take the day off. Grandad often told the story of a Good Friday trip to London, concerning some Hanham Colliers.

On arrival, after a welcome relaxation at the 'Load of Hay' the colliers decided to visit Madame Tussaud's Waxworks. One of the men who had been drinking hard, had what his mates were pleased to call 'a skinfull'. He became very annoyed with a well-known waxwork figure, that of an elderly lady whose head moved continually from side to side, giving the impression of her distinct disapproval of all who dared to look at her.

The man by this time was bleary-eyed and he pushed his head forward, then raised a clenched fist saying, "Who bis thee shakin' thee 'ead at? I get enough of that from my old woman."

But still the offending head continued to shake, "I ain't telling thee agen," shouted the collier. "If thou dussunt stop, I'll hit thee 'ead off."

Of course the head still went on moving from side to side. The collier promptly knocked it off.

The management demanded £5 for the damage, but as he had no money left his mates had to subscribe.

Three

Staple Hill – The final hymn for a stricken giant – Downend – Graceful humour

Staple Hill

Before the County of Avon came into being, Staple Hill was in South Gloucestershire and the atmosphere was rather like that of a country market town, with the countryside on its doorstep. Here, shopkeepers and customers referred to each other by their Christian names, and everyone seemed to know everyone else.

Staple Hill once had its own fire brigade and in the days before its mechanisation they used to put their horses to graze in Page Park, so when a fire broke out they had first to catch the horse.

In the early twentieth century the Staple Hill Fire Brigade used horse-drawn vehicles to transport them to fires.

One of the most prominent buildings in Staple Hill is Hebron Methodist Church built in 1874. Its forerunner still stands further along the High Street, but is now two buildings and hardly recognisable.

16

The Chapel was known as 'Bethlehem', and there is a story about a visiting Evangelist preacher, a dwarf, who had to stand on a stool in the pulpit because he was so small. He had just got to the point in his sermon where he warned the congregation that the unrighteous would be cast down into the lower regions when, due to his excited gesticulation, the stool tipped over and he disappeared from view.

At the beginning of this century the local Salvation Army sent a contingent down to Fishponds every Sunday. It was led by the 'Army' brass band, and is said to have marched down the hill, headed by the conductor, a one-legged man who on the occasions when the 'beat' flagged, walked backwards, frantically waving his baton.

Staple Hill's earliest industries have now died out or moved away, with the exception of a thriving clothing manufacture. The last few years of the nineteenth century saw the end of a pin-making industry. The last pin-factory to close was at Lower Station Road, Staple Hill. Production ceased after the death of the proprietor, Mr Thomas Rawbone, and the premises lay idle for many years. Then in 1937, the factory suddenly sprang into the news and Bristol newspapers labelled it as 'Rip Van Winkle Factory', 'Spectre of a Dead Industry' and 'Pin Factory for Sale'.

The factory had remained untouched for almost 40 years, just as the last of the pin-makers had left it. Brass wire was still threaded in the machines, and there were half-filled boxes of pins lying about.

On hearing that the premises were being auctioned Mr H.W. Maxwell, Curator of Bristol Museum, went along to view the contents and obtained some pin-making machines. Having got more than he required, he sold two of them to Gloucester Museum for ten shillings (50p).

Overlooking Page Park stands Hill House, a Georgian mansion now converted to luxury flats. It has a claim to fame. One of its owners, Alderman John Haythorne, lived here at the beginning of the nineteenth century. During one of his terms of office as Mayor of Bristol he was privately visited by the Prince Regent, later King George IV.

Public benefactor Handel Cossham once lived at Hill House. He owned many coal-mines in the area and left in his will funds to build Cossham Hospital. Later, another public benefactor, Alderman A.J. Page, lived in the house and he bequeathed Page Park for the enjoyment of all.

The final hymn for a stricken giant

Of all the true stories and legends that have sprung from the sinking of the *Titanic*, few have caught the imagination more than the account of the ship's band playing hymns as the water lapped around their feet. It somehow summarises the stiff-upper-lip spirit which we are led to believe prevailed to the end.

The man at the centre of it all was a popular Bristolian, well known for his evangelistic work in the east of the city.

Robert Bateman, Uncle Bob to hundreds of Bristol children in the teeming city suburbs, was the son of a Staple Hill mason. He had a way with words and when he went to America to pursue his evangelistic work, he already had a powerful reputation as a local preacher. When he returned to Bristol in 1912 to organise a headstone for his mother's grave at Downend, it was as Mayor of Florida.

While on this visit to Bristol, he conducted a mission at Kingswood Evangel Hall and when he was due to return to America, the Evangel Mission Hall's brass band led a procession of 100 people to escort him to Staple Hill Railway Station.

As his train pulled out, a member of the band ran to the end of the platform, and on his euphonium gave a rendering of 'Rocked in the Cradle of the Deep'. This musician, Mr E.T. Cozens, later Alderman of the City of Bristol, little realised at the time that events would prove it to have been an almost unbearably poignant farewell.

Once on board the *Titanic* at Southampton Bob Bateman soon became known to Captain Edward Smith, who asked him to conduct a Sunday Service. The Captain promised the services of the band, a crack line-up which was as proficient playing hymns as it was in pounding out the hit song of the year, 'Alexander's Ragtime Band'.

When disaster struck and the *Titanic* hit an iceberg Bob Bateman's first thoughts were not for music but for his sister-in-law, travelling with him to see his wife. He threw her unceremoniously into a lifeboat, and only then did he return to the band, calling on it to play 'Nearer my God to Thee'. This was taken up by the passengers and crew who had been unable to escape in lifeboats and still on the *Titanic* were awaiting the end.

Just before the vessel's final hideous plunge, Bob Bateman

requested 'Abide with me' and he was still beating time to the tune when he was washed overboard.

His frozen body was recovered some time later. The Public Archives of Nova Scotia records his body as having been picked up by the cable ship s.s. *Mackay-Bennett*, named Robert Bateman, (per) Pendennis, Staple Hill, Bristol. His body was claimed by his widow, Mrs Bateman of Jacksonville, Florida.

But for the rest of their lives, those who saw him off from the noisy Staple Hill Railway Station, must have remembered that lone figure playing 'Rocked in the Cradle of the Deep', as a hand waved to them from the moving train and then was gone.

Downend

Downend was once part of Mangotsfield but was separated when Christ Church was opened in 1831. Its first encumbent was the Rev. Alfred Peache, from whom a road in the district takes its name.

In the churchyard some eminent worthies of the Victorian era are buried.

Joseph Croot was laid to rest in 1899. He was the last Town Crier of Bristol to be appointed to that ancient office which lapsed about 1891. When carrying out his duties he wore a black livery coat with buttons bearing the Bristol Coat of Arms, a tricorn hat, blue velvet breeches, gaiters, and flowers in his lapel.

This jolly gentleman would deliver his O-yez O-yez with his script in one hand and a mug of 'what he fancied' in the other.

Then there lies Alfred Pocock who is credited with having instructed the Grace family in 'the art of cricket' and Rev. Emlyn Jones who wrote his enlightening book on Downend and Mangotsfield history. In this, amongst other things, he informs us about the famous Downend 'teas' of long ago. These were presided over by Julia Peache whose husband, the Rev. Alfred Peache was noted for the humorous speeches he gave on these occasions.

There is a lady who lies close to the church, Miss Frances Anne Cooper, who died in 1880 at the age of 88 years. For more than 40 years she was schoolmistress of the little Mangotsfield schoolhouse which stands opposite 'The Red Lion' public house.

One very windy morning Miss Cooper left her home and set off as

19

usual for the schoolhouse. It was slow progress however, as this prim Victorian school teacher struggled along the lane clutching her bonnet, while at the same time frantically trying to hold down her voluminous petticoats in a vain attempt not to show her pantalets.

She began to feel that she was fighting a losing battle when suddenly there was a very strong gust of wind which caused her petticoats to billow out like an umbrella. So small and lightweight was she that it lifted her off her feet and she was blown across the lane into a pool of water.

Fortunately someone had seen the occurrence, and swiftly came to her aid. With her teeth chattering and her corkscrew curls now straight, she was taken back to the house where she lived with Mrs Wilmot. This good lady no doubt put her to bed with a drink of something 'that really warmed her up'.

There was no school that day, much to the delight of her pupils whom she ruled with strict discipline, in spite of her diminutive appearance.

Downend as seen by Samuel Loxton around 1919.

Graceful Humour

Most towns, suburbs and villages have stories of their favourite families, past or present. At Downend we have the Grace family who have often been credited with humorous anecdotes.

George Pocock was the maternal grandfather of the famous cricketer Dr W.G. Grace. He was a man 'who wore several hats', one as a Methodist itinerant preacher, another as a schoolmaster, and a third as an inventor.

The pupils of Mr Pocock's school for 'Sons of Gentlemen' were certainly never bored, since the boys never knew what their worthy schoolmaster would be doing next. For instance, one day he introduced his pupils to his early brainchild, 'The Spanking Machine', a contraption which consisted of a rotating wheel with a number of dummy hands attached, which in turn slapped the hapless wrong-doer.

Then there was a period when he disdained the services of a horsedrawn carriage and, instead, attached powerful kites to the carriage and drove all the way from Bristol to London by wind-power.

George Pocock was quite an authority on wind-power and carried out many experiments with kites. He caused a great sensation when he tried to interest the Admiralty in a device to save the survivors of shipwrecks by using kite-power to carry them from ship to shore.

It was a great day for Mr Pocock's pupils when they assembled on Clifton Down along with many other Bristolians, to witness one of his inventions. Very confidently he placed his daughter Martha in a kitchen chair and attached a huge magnificent kite to it. The kite was loosened and Martha swung out into the air and over the cliffs of the Avon Gorge. She landed safely, appearing to be none the worse for her adventure.

Martha Pocock later became the mother of the great cricketer, Dr W.G. Grace. It's a sobering thought that the mere existence of her cricketing family literally hung by a string.

When W.G.'s brother Dr Henry Grace left their Downend home he established a practice at Hanham, and took charge of the local cricket team, often inviting W.G. to play with them.

A match was organised between Dr Henry's side, and Bitton cricket club. The two brothers had just stowed their gear in to the

21

pony trap and were about to set off for Bitton, when their brother Edward also tossed his gear in.

According to an onlooker, there was an expression of doubt on the brothers' faces, and W.G. was heard to say, "Bitton won't stand for it Ted – not the three of us against them."

They arrived at the Bitton ground and, much to the surprise of W.G. and Henry, the Bitton players greeted Edward like a long-lost brother. His well-kept secret was now out – Edward had agreed to play for Bitton.

The game progressed long and leisurely, reaching a point where there were only ten runs between the two sides. The crowd was shouting for decisive action, complaining that they hadn't seen a decent hit all day.

In cocksure manner Edward called out saying "I'll soon remedy that."

Dr Henry delivered a nice easy ball, Edward took a mighty swing with his bat . . . and missed. Hanham won.

Dr Henry was a man loved and respected, and he inspired confidence in his patients. There is a story of a Kingswood woman who called on Dr Henry and declared, "I got the Devil in I, an' I do want for 'ee to cure me." Another doctor would have probably told her to go away and not waste his time. But Dr Henry was something of a psychologist. He could also speak the local dialect, and said to the woman, "Put out thee tongue Missus, an' let I feel thee pulse." The woman did as she was told, then Dr Henry said, "I can see what's the matter. I'll make some lotion for you. Now when you get home, put your finger in it, if it comes out black, that's the sign that the Devil is gone."

The woman went away firmly believing that Dr Grace could work a miracle. The next day she was back again at his surgery absolutely delighted. "I done what you towld I," she said "an' a girt black cross came out, – an' the Devil's gone. Thank 'ee Dr Grace."

22

Cricketing Grace brothers: Dr W.G. (sitting) and Henry (standing).

Four

Fishponds – The Old French Prison – Wickham Court – Stand and Deliver

Fishponds

Fishponds was formerly in the Parish of Stapleton; on ancient maps of the area it is marked as 'New Pools'.

There were two pools, separated by a highway; one was situated near the Full Moon Hotel, before it was filled in. The other pool was on the opposite side of the road, it too was filled in, by order of the Duchess of Beaufort after a child had fallen in and drowned.

The stretch of road which ran between the pools and along to The Cross Hands Hotel is now known as the Straits, and its name is subject to much discussion.

One story says that it got its name towards the end of the eighteenth century when the Prince Regent, later King George IV, and the Duke of Beaufort were riding along this particular stretch of the highway. At that time the road was bending and twisting and full of potholes and His Royal Highness, being jolted from one side of the coach to the other, could contain his wrath no longer. According to legend he bellowed loudly, "Beaufort! Make this road straight, and I'll give you the land on each side."

The Duke was said to have obeyed His Royal Highness, and also, to have kept him to his word.

Alongside Fishponds Park is a building which was originally erected to incorporate the village school, the schoolmaster's house and an alms-house for four old women.

The eighteenth century celebrity Hannah More was born in the schoolmaster's house, her father being the schoolmaster. A plaque there commemorates her birth in 1745.

In spite of her humble beginnings, Hannah More climbed the ladder of success to become accepted in London's most brilliant literary circle. She was a friend of Dr Johnson, David Garrick and Lord Macaulay and also had duchesses as friends. She made a fortune from her writings and eventually made her home at Cowslip Green, Wrington. Religion at the time being at a low ebb, she stirred

24

Hannah More by John Opie, 1787.

up the church around the Cheddar and the Chew Valley areas by doing work to alleviate the poverty in the Mendip villages.

Opposite Fishponds Park once stood another residence which in its latter years was known as 'Beechwood'. It had an impressive list of occupiers such as James Brydges, a kinsman of the Duke of Chandos, and William Edward Forster, who was responsible for the Education Bill of 1870.

The main village pump once stood in Station Road. John Wesley is recorded to have lodged near this pump, and one wonders if his famous words 'Cleanliness is next to Godliness', may first have occurred to him as he watched the Fishponds ladies as they gathered around the pump to draw water.

One of the most picturesque of Fishponds houses was Oldbury Court which overlooked the Frome valley. It is shown on a map of 1610 and might well have been one of the hunting lodges used by King John when he hunted in the Kingswood Forest.

Fishponds lost its great antiquity when Oldbury Court was demolished in the 1950s, and became Vassal's Park open to the public.

Oldbury Court was said to have had its ghosts. One ghost was that of a Roman Catholic Priest, who had hidden in a secret room, and for some unknown reason had been unable to get out again. He was said to have haunted the house, and even after it was demolished, it has been claimed that the ghost of the priest has been seen in Vassal's Park.

Oldbury Court was reputedly haunted, and even after its demolition people have claimed to have seen a ghost on the site.

Fishponds has been associated with mental health since the eighteenth century when Dr Mason, a resident of Beechwood, built an asylum at Fishponds and bequeathed it to his grandson Dr Joseph Mason Cox. He went into partnership with Dr George Bompass.

In 1746 Bristol's Town Clerk and two of his own clerks were said to have become mentally disturbed in the same week and were lodged at this asylum.

There were many complaints concerning the state of affairs at this institution and an enquiry was set up.

The Dower House at Stapleton, locally known as 'The Duchesses' was purchased from the Duke of Beaufort in 1907 by Harold Nelson Burden, a pioneer in mental health, and in 1909 he founded Stoke Park Colony, centred around the Dower House.

There is a pictorial record of the Dower House on a Wedgewood plate. Wedgewood Pottery made a 952 piece dinner and desert service for Empress Catherine II of Russia and the Dower House was one of the scenes. It is strange to think that this bit of the Stapleton scene is displayed in The Winter Garden Palace, Leningrad.

The Old French Prison

Manor Park Hospital, Fishponds stands on the site of an old French prison which was built in 1779 to house naval prisoners of war. Britain at that time was at war with the American Colonies, France and Spain, and Holland a little later.

The Admiralty regulations concerning the prisoners, their food and living conditions, were certainly humane but unfortunately were seldom enforced. Unscrupulous agents who were contracted to supply food and other requirements deprived the prisoners of their due but charged the Admiralty for the specified amount.

When hostilities between Britain and her enemies ceased for a while, the building was used for training boys in the art of seamanship. But war broke out again and the building was once more filled with prisoners of war and the old rogues who had deprived the prisoners were back in business.

In spite of building extensions the prison became overcrowded as more and more prisoners were brought in. Hammocks were slung in three tiers with only 18 inches between. The windows were bolted and barred at night to prevent escapes, and this lack of ventilation, especially in summer, spread disease. The original toilets were described as being 'open necessary tubs'. John Howard, the prison reformer, was asked how he managed to avoid infection from such unhealthy conditions when he made his visits. He said, "I trust in divine providence, but I never enter a prison before breakfast, and in an offensive room I seldom breathe deeply."

There was a lack of sufficient water at the prison. Clothing was supposed to be supplied by the prisoners own governments, but the French Government failed to supply their men. Prisoners were found to be almost naked and many without shoes. Enforced idleness led to quarrels and duels between the Frenchmen, and gambling resulted in clothes changing hands.

Visits from well meaning citizens were banned. John Wesley wrote religious tracts for the prisoners but these were not allowed under the rule that "intrigue, enticements and force may not be used to oblige any prisoner to change his religion."

Food in the prison was not only scarce but rotten and unfit for human consumption. Things reached such a state that local people dared not let their dogs stray to the prison in case they became dog soup the next day. Food given to sick prisoners was said to have been hardly fit for dogs.

Rumours of semi-starvation were investigated by two Bristol merchants, who found prisoners to be pale, emaciated, and appearing to be dying of famine, almost reduced to skeletons.

Six to eight prisoners died each day, deaths being caused by bad food, scabies, scurvy and typhus and at one point smallpox had broken out. There were also violent deaths.

The Gloucestershire Coroner complained bitterly of the extra work of having to hold so many inquests. Many burials took place in the grounds.

With the expectation of a French invasion in 1797 came the barbarous suggestion of confining the prisoners in local coal-pits. Fortunately the invasion never took place.

The French prisoners were very clever with their hands and carved articles from bone and wood, such as bodkins, tatting needles, dice, chessmen and dominoes etc. They also made model ships with exquisite workmanship and paid great attention to detail. Prison markets were held within the outer walls of the prison, where the prisoners were able to sell things they had made.

The Peace Treaty of Paris, brought the release of 2,000 prisoners from the Stapleton Prison, the longest serving being the first to go.

The last 600 men were marched in two divisions via Hanham and Keynsham and then on to Portsmouth, because the transport department objected to the heavy dock dues at Pill. Some however were sent down the River Avon, being too sick to travel with the others. Seven were taken to Bristol Royal Infirmary, and the last prisoner was taken to the Fishponds poorhouse. By 1865 the Old French Prison was demolished.

Wickham Court

Wickham Court, an ancient Stapleton house, played an important role during the Civil War.

Over the doorway is a plaque which bears the inscription –
"Wickham Court"
Oliver Cromwell and General Fairfax
held a Council of War in this house
before the attack on Bristol
in September 1645.

It's not difficult to imagine the scene which took place here in the autumn of long ago, when the country folk living in this quiet valley were agog with excitement.

Groups of dusty infantry and cavalry streamed down the lane to Wickham Court, the horses sweating and the men's uniforms spattered with mud.

On arriving at the Court sentries were detailed to their postings on high ground, some to the slope, now Manor Park Road, others to outposts set up on the other side of the river and some near Stapleton Church where they looked longingly at the open door of the nearby inn while on duty.

At the riverside a group of musketry rested by the buttresses of the grey stone pack-horse bridge, where the ground was damp and the trees silently dropped their yellowing leaves into the deep water below, no doubt wondering when they were going to get their next meal.

29

Meanwhile Oliver Cromwell and General Fairfax, together with their officers, dined before planning their campaign to take Bristol.

There seems to have been a clash between Cromwell and Fairfax on the subject of strategy whether "to endeavour to block the City, or to make a regular seige". In the words of Cromwell,

> "We had a Council of War concerning the storming of the town, about eight days before we took it, and in that, there appeared to be great unwillingness to work, through the weather being unreasonable."

A little further down the River Frome is an outcrop of rock which, although reddish in colour, is known as 'The Black Rocks' owing to an old legend which tells of a tragedy which took place there hundreds of years ago.

At Wickham Court there lived a young lady who was betrothed to an adventurous young man who was often absent for long periods of time. There came a time when he was away so long that she thought he no longer cared for her, and as a result she became ill and listless.

Eventually, tired of his wanderings, he returned to Wickham Court one night. It was late and all was quiet. He knocked several times, but receiving no response, and not wishing to disturb the residents from their slumbers, he went off to take shelter for the night in a cave beneath the rocks.

After he had been sleeping for a while, he suddenly awoke, for there was a sound of moaning in the chill night air. He listened intently and heard the sound again. Then coming out of the cave into the moonlight, he looked up to the rocks high above him. There he saw a figure clothed in white.

He thought at first it was a spirit, but as it did not fade away he clambered up the rocks. There to his astonishment was the lady to whom he was betrothed. Her eyes were open, but unseeing. He called her name but, too late, he realised that she was sleep-walking.

She awoke with a start, swayed, then fell over the edge of the rock and slid into the dark waters below.

The river bore her downstream, and he ran along the bank catching up with her as her hair became entangled in a branch of a tree which was trailing in the water.

Carrying her body to Wickham Court, he left her with the sorrowing household. The legend says that he lived out the rest of his life as a hermit in a cave in the Avon Gorge.

Wickham Court

Stand and Deliver

At the beginning of the last century the roadway from Stapleton Church to Eastville was heavily shaded with trees and frequented by highwaymen. The story goes that a farm labourer travelling this way home, was stopped by the command, "Stand and deliver." The man stopped fearfully; he had his weekly wages in his pocket, which he was forced to hand over. Realising that there was now no money what-so-ever with which to face the week ahead, he begged and implored the highwaymen to give him back at least a few coppers to buy bread.

This must have struck a sympathetic cord in one of the highwaymen, for he thrust his hand into his pouch, threw a few coins on the ground and rode away. It was almost dark, and they were quickly out of sight. The labourer went home to tell his wife the sad news, and laid the coins on the table.

As the candle-light shone on them, to his great joy, he saw that they were eight golden sovereigns.

Perhaps in his haste and the falling darkness, the highwayman got his coins mixed up, or maybe he had a good day, and pangs of conscience had caused him to take pity on the labourer, and to give him a real helping hand.

Five

Baptist Mills – Watercress Farm – Easton

Baptist Mills

The ancient Roman road which ran from the River Severn to Bath crossed the River Frome at a point near The Old Fox Inn. Before the construction of the motorway the inn stood near the river in the Baptist Mills district. It was built around the beginning of the eighteenth century, and as an added attraction to its normal facilities, provided a bathing place, 'complete with dressing houses'. In the eighteenth and nineteenth centuries the whole area seems to have been something of a pleasure ground where bare-fisted prize-fighters displayed their prowess, and cock-fighting was a great attraction.

The mill from which the Baptist Mills area takes its name was called Bagpath's by William Worcester in 1480. But by 1610 its name was changed to Baptist Mill. This was nearly half a century before the rise of the English Baptists and it has been suggested that French Huguenot Weavers had occupied the mill and produced 'baptiste' or cambric weave.

It was on this mill site that in 1702 Abraham Darby set up a brassworks and also produced cast-iron pots. His Quaker partners however, did not share his enthusiasm for ironware so he moved to Coalbrookdale in 1709, and founded his famous iron-works. Meanwhile, his partners extended their brass production at Baptist Mills where, according to an industrial spy, they had 25 furnaces.

In the 1970s a Bristol roofing firm had their works on the mill site, and traces of the mill could still be seen.

At the junction of Mina Road and Warwick Road there stood a Weslyan Chapel, and behind it a building which was once a bakery. According to a local story, this was run by a resourceful baker.

Due to the poor state of his oven, the loaves were often a little burnt and flattened, so the baker sold his bread for a little less than was usual. The local housewives grumbled but accepted this state of affairs as they were allowed to roast their Sunday meat and bake their apple pies in his oven free of charge.

After many years of serving the local community there came a time when baking was brought to a standstill as the stone floor of his oven was broken beyond repair. Stone could have been purchased and a mason paid to shape it to size, but as he was by no means a wealthy man this would have been too expensive, and he could not afford to be out of production.

So he did a little local investigation, then waited until dusk, when he and his two hefty sons crept into the churchyard, and they heaved out two of the smaller tombstones. These flat stones were quickly fitted into the floor of the oven and cemented into position. They worked in dim light and in a great hurry, failing to notice that one of the stones faced upwards with a little of its epitaph showing.

The next morning the smell of newly-baked bread wafted in the breeze. The loaves were delivered rather late that morning, and the baker got more than the usual amount of grumbles. But very soon both adults and children were busy holding up the warm crusty loaves to the mirror in order to read the words which appeared thereon.

"He has risen".

This swiftly became regarded as the baker's guarantee and from then on he never dared to deliver an unsatisfactory loaf.

Watercress Farm

It's difficult to imagine the St Werburgh's area being referred to as 'out in the country', and a much favoured rendezvous for Bristolians of Victorian times.

Passing along Mina Road and through the long railway arch just beyond St Werburgh's Church, there was, in those days, a very pleasant spot set amid lush meadowland where cattle grazed and where the slopes of Ashley Hill were still green downland. There was a cornmill and a millhouse. The millwheel was motivated by tumbling falls of springwater which took rise in the hill, and in the foam-flecked waters grew masses of tender green watercress said to have been the best flavoured cress in the West country.

On sunny weekends and warm summer evenings it attracted many visitors. It was a great place for picnics and strolling through the woods. Bowls and skittles were played in the grounds of the nearby tavern, while the less energetic were served with watercress teas, for which the tavern was famous.

Today, it is 'The Farm' and in the bar hang photographs of the inn when it was known as South Wales Railway Tavern.

Easton

The Roman Road which crossed the River Frome near 'The Old Fox' can be traced over to Easton near St Mark's Church.

In 1875, workmen laying water mains discovered a hoard of Roman coins which they were said to have carried away 'in bowler-hat fulls' and so Easton has its 'Roman Road'.

Almost opposite The Queen's Head Inn, there once stood a house with a blacksmith's attached. The house was known as 'Churchill' and probably built around the end of the sixteenth century. It was said to have been the oldest in Easton. The blacksmith's was even older.

The buildings were probably once part of a forest lodge, where the smithy could attend to the shoeing of the huntsmen's horses, and perhaps provide their arrows.

An old map of the area marks the spot as a 'hunting box' and the historian Seyer tells of King John riding out to Easton, where he then entered the Forest through a gateway.

Some years ago Mr George Burchell, an organist of the now-demolished Easton Road Methodist Chapel, said that he had once seen the deeds of the first house in the nearby Tyndalls Park Road, (Easton) this house was known as 'Lawnwood' and its garden ran behind the Chapel. On the deed of the house was the drawing of a gate and bore the words 'Entrance to the Kingswood Forest.'

The house appeared to be eighteenth century. It was demolished and I was informed that the deeds of its land were with The Bristol Omnibus Company.

Six

The Blue Bowl Inn – Tom Cribb – The man who saved the Flying Dutchman – The Don John Cross

The Blue Bowl Inn

Legend has it that the Blue Bowl Inn, Hanham is one of the oldest pubs in Britain. The inn stands on the old Roman road, sometimes referred to as the Via Julia, which runs from the River Severn to Bath. The inn is believed to have once been a Roman tavern which served the soldiers of The Second Legion Augusta and a hoard of Roman coins found nearby and other Roman finds in Hanham gives credence to this story.

The first real evidence of the inn's antiquity comes from the writings of St Lyte who, in 1480, mentions the inn as an old established hostelry. The pub appears again later in history when Oliver Cromwell and some of his officers were billeted there for a few nights, and the main contingent of his troops camped at a place later to be known as 'Troopers Hill'.

In the eighteenth century John Wesley, the great religious reformer, stayed in a house near the Blue Bowl Inn on his visits to the Kingswood area.

Members of the Cock Road Gang who held sway in Kingswood and Hanham area in the late eighteenth and early nineteenth centuries, patronised the Blue Bowl Inn. But one of their number known as 'Dick Boy' must have been the least welcome, for it is said that when he stayed overnight he would get into bed with his boots on in order to make a quick get-a-way if necessary. No doubt he hardly endeared himself to the landlord's wife.

It's not known how long this inn has been called the Blue Bowl Inn but it may have come from a man called Edward Bye, who lived there more than 200 years ago. He worked at the Brislington Pottery which made Bristol Delft Ware and here he produced a special 'Blue Bowl' of fine workmanship.

There is a story still told in Hanham today, that when Prince

35

Philip was stationed at Corsham he was 'down' to play for a darts team. The match was due to be held at the Blue Bowl Inn. But the fixture clashed with the date of his marriage to her Royal Highness The Princess Elizabeth.

This inn was patronised by Tom Cribb, England's champion prize-fighter, whose special mug was kept on a hook near the bar.

A Victorian painting of the Blue Bowl Inn, reputed to be one of the oldest pubs in Britain.

Tom Cribb

Jefferies Hill, Hanham was once the scene of many prize-fights, and was probably the early training ground of Tom Cribb, who excelled in this sport to reach the height of this profession.

Born in Hanham on July 8th, 1781, he was the son of Hannah and Thomas Cribb. His father worked in a Hanham quarry, and as a boy young Tom did too. However, he was soon to 'conquer fresh fields' and he became a sailor and served his country.

The stamina and toughness he acquired in the quarries and as a sailor put Tom in good stead for becoming a fighter. He was first recognised as a prize-fighter when he beat George Maddox in 1805.

At this time, the Bristol area seems to have been the breeding ground for great prize-fighters. There was Jem Belcher born in Bristol in the same year as Tom, Bob Britton, and the Bristolian Henry Pearce, also known as 'Hen Pearce' and so became known as 'The Game Chicken'. He beat the now one-eyed Jem Belcher and so assumed the Champion's laurels. He retired undefeated, winning his last fight against John Gully, who was born at the 'Rose and Crown', Wick.

The Championship became vacant and was contended by John Gully and Bob Gregson. Gully was the winner and, like Pearce, retired an undefeated Champion. He later became a Member of Parliament.

By this time Tom Cribb was coming to the fore. He beat Jem Belcher in a terrific battle and, with Gully now out of the game, he fought Bob Gregson for the Championship, and won. Tom was then challenged by Jem Belcher but Tom won and Jem's fighting days were over.

Tom Cribb of Hanham was now undisputed Champion of England. Then came a new challenger, from America. He was Tom Molyneux, a former negro slave who had gained his freedom by winning a fight on which his master had wagered a very large sum, and who had come to England to seek his fortune.

The fight between the English Champion and this Champion of America was regarded as the Championship of the World.

The fight took place on December 18th, 1810. It was hard fought and took its toll on both men. Both were physically exhausted, but kept fighting until finally Molyneux conceded he could fight no more. But the closeness of the struggle encouraged Molyneux to issue another challenge. Cribb responded by vigorous training for the re-match, but Molyneux neglected to do so. The fight took place on September 28th, 1811, and was watched by something like 20,000 people.

Tom Cribb was an easy winner, and on his arrival in London a couple of days later he received great public ovation at Holborn, which was rendered almost impassable by the crowds assembled there.

37

In 1821 it was decided that Tom Cribb, having held the championship for ten years without being challenged, could not be expected to fight any more and therefore would remain Champion for the rest of his life.

In the same year Tom Cribb, dressed as a page, was among the prize-fighters who stood guard at Westminster Hall at the Coronation of King George IV.

The man who saved the Flying Dutchman

John Chiddy was a Hanham man who is commemorated for a very brave deed which thrilled not only the Bristol area but the whole nation.

It took place when he was working at a quarry siding on the St Anne's side of the River Avon.

The *Flying Dutchman* was one of the fastest trains in the world in the 1870s, with a top speed of around 60 miles an hour. This express train ran from London, through Bristol to Exeter and every effort was made by the officials on the line to ensure safety during its rapid journey. But on March 31st, 1876 at about 2.20pm, when the train was within two miles of Bristol, a terrible accident seemed imminent. On an open stretch of line between Brunel's two tunnels a large stone had fallen on to the track.

Close by was Birchwood Quarry and, as was usual practice, quarried stone had been stacked near the track ready for loading on to a freight train. On this occasion however one of these stones became dislodged from the stack, and rolled down on to the track.

It was fortunate for the passengers on the express train that one of the workers at the quarry, John Chiddy, saw the stone. If the train had hit the stone and derailed, the train would have plummetted 20 feet down into the River Avon – a major disaster. Chiddy was fully aware that the *Flying Dutchman* was due at any moment and seeing the stone he made a dash for this very large boulder and with superhuman effort managed to push it clear of the line.

But the train was bearing down on him at 50 miles per hour and it hit and killed him instantly, throwing him some nine yards down the track. Chiddy was 47 years of age and left a widow and seven or eight children unprovided for.

Chiddy's bravery was reported and commented upon in almost every newspaper in the country and it was recognised that he saved not only the train, but also the lives of the passengers. An appeal was launched for subscriptions to provide funds for the widow and family who were so suddenly deprived of their bread winner. But a meagre sum of only £3.2s was collected, despite the fact the train was filled with passengers.

This heroic deed became the main topic of conversation in east Bristol throughout the summer, and there was great regret that there appeared to be no compensation payable.

The case was taken up by Lord Elcho, a Member of Parliament, and in August of 1876 he told the House of Commons the whole story of John Chiddy who "by great promptitude and energy" managed to remove a large stone from the path of the oncoming *Flying Dutchman*, and in all probability had averted a great catastrophe. But it was at the cost of his own life, and had left his family destitute.

Lord Elcho continued,

> Bravery in the field is recognised by The Victoria Cross, and at sea, by The Albert Medal and if a civilian is called upon to perform such an act of bravery, it ought to be recognised . . .

In view of the great publicity given to the case, and because it had been an issue in the House of Commons, the prominent citizens of Bristol were impelled to call a meeting for the purpose of starting a Chiddy Memorial Fund. The meeting was held in September of the same year, and it was decided to buy a plot of land and to build a house upon it.

In 1877 the Chiddy Memorial Cottage was built on a spot which, at that time, gave a clear view of the site where the brave deed took place, and was one of the most picturesque spots along the River Avon. The key of Memorial Cottage was handed to John Chiddy's widow on January 8th, 1878. In 1926 Memorial Road in Hanham was named after him.

Nature has healed the scars in the landscape made by Birchwood and other quarries along the banks of the Avon but the open track between Brunel's tunnels will go down in the annals of The Great Western Railway as the scene of remarkable courage.

John Chiddy's Memorial Cottage, by Samuel Loxton.

The Don John Cross

The Don John Cross was once a significant landmark of the Kingswood Forest and was said to have stood at the junction of the Hanham and Kingswood roads near St George Fountain. This stone structure had, over many centuries, served as a shrine, a boundary. and resting place for many a weary traveller.

An old legend tells that a bier bearing the body of a Spanish nobleman rested at the cross for a brief spell before resuming its journey. Hence it acquired the name 'Don John Cross'.

It must have been a familiar landmark to Thomas Putley, a keeper of the Kingswood Forest. He died in 1596 and was laid to rest in the Church of St Philip and Jacob. The marks of his calling, a dog and crossbow, are carved on his tomb.

In the seventeenth century the cross, known at this time as Dungeon's Cross, was mentioned in court in the case of 'The Crown versus The Liberty Owners'. Richard Prosser is recorded as having said:

> All the passengers passing Roegate and Dungeon's Cross with wains and pack saddles pay a penny for every pack saddle and fourpence for every wain or cart.

A Bristol Journal dated January 1749, reported that

> Rural labourers styling themselves as Jack-O-Lents' being furious at the levying of tolls, tore down the gates near the Don John Cross.

As the years wore on this once-revered cross, like many other wayside crosses, became a place where the superstitious preferred not to linger once the daylight hours had passed. For up until 1823, it was the custom to bury malefactors and suicides at the crossroads.

In 1728 a newspaper reported:

> The shoe-maker that hanged himself without Lawford's Gate was buried in the crossroad called Dungel's Cross. We hear that some young surgeons have since caused him to be taken up again and anatomised.

In his *History of The Bristol Royal Infirmary*, G. Munro Smith M.D. tells the story of Long Jack, a well-known vagabond who committed suicide by cutting his throat and was buried at the cross. Abraham Ludlow, a surgeon, and three others dug up his body and took it to Ludlow's house in the town. It was discovered by a serving maid who recognised the body as that of Long Jack and ran into the street screaming and telling what she had seen. Anticipating that her story would cause trouble, Ludlow and his companions returned Long Jack to the cross.

It was just as well they did as a number of Jack's cronies went to the crossroads to see if Long Jack was still buried there, vowing vengeance if they didn't find him. A few strokes from the pick-axe relieved their doubts as Long Jack's spindly legs came into view.

Seven

The Netham Works

Standing at the Netham Lock and looking across to Barton Hill, it is difficult to imagine that a large industrial complex, known locally as The Chemical Works, once stood here. In about 1817, the chemical business was transferred from Oldland to the Netham, where it was run under various partnerships until it was registered as the Netham Chemical Company, and later the United Alkali Company. The works finally closed in 1949.

This one-time industry has now vanished from the Netham as though it never existed, but at its peak the works on the north bank of the feeder between Blackswarth Road and the Marsh Lane Bridge covered about 65 acres.

When owned by the United Alkali Company, its landmark was a gigantic chimney which reared 300 feet above ground and puffed out great clouds of smoke. It stood for some 80 years before its demolition in 1950 and quite a few stories can be told about this 'Netham Monster'.

The chimney was estimated to have been constructed with about one million bricks, and the demolition firm claimed that it was the largest stack that had been felled in this country at that time.

A few years earlier the demolition foreman had been called in to repair the stack and when he was almost at the top, it was struck by lightning. His hair was singed, but miraculously he escaped unhurt.

Mr Frank Windsor who worked at the Netham for 36 years said he recalled only four fatalities during his time; the first occurred

The Netham Works, by Samuel Loxton.

when a man who was waiting with a steel pin to couple a Straker Squire waggon and trailer together was crushed between the two. The second fatality was caused when a tram of hot saltcake fell on a worker, and a third fell through the roof of a high building. Another was killed by an electric current; two men were working on a winch lowering a steel girder when it touched a power cable. One of them was safe in rubbersoled footwear, but the other was wearing hob-nail boots.

Charlie Adamson also had memories. "When the night shift knocked off at six o'clock in the morning, some of us used to go to Beek's public house at the top of Netham Lane. We ate sandwiches and pork pies, and swilled them down with beer – very welcome and necessary too, after sweating in front of hot furnaces for the whole shift. We had to drink hard to put back moisture into our bodies."

The Netham works was self-sufficient; it had various forms of transport including a fleet of Straker Squire steam driven waggons, tipping lorries and small two-wheeled cars used on the premises for lighter work. It had its own fleet of barges, named after exotic gemstones – *Ruby*, *Diamond*, *Pearl*, *Beryl* and *Onyx*. These were towed by a steam tug, *The Ibex*. Trams carried the goods from the storesheds down to the awaiting barges. They were worked on an endless chain system with a wheel at the top of the incline and another at the bottom near the barges. The barges then took the finished products to the docks and returned with raw materials. There were always people on the banks of the waterway watching these operations with great interest.

The works also had its own blacksmiths, plumbers, brick-layers and other tradesmen. The rural craft of basket-making was practised here, as baskets were in constant demand to hold the acid-filled glass car-boys.

Many leisure hours were spent in the firm's gymnasium, which was well equipped and included a full size boxing ring. Then there was the annual fruit, flower and vegetable show for employees and their families and on bank holidays there were boat trips up the River Avon to Hanham and Keynsham tea-gardens.

The area on which the Netham chemical works stood is now grassed over, and time is erasing the memories of those who spent their working lives there.

Eight

St Anne's – Crew's Hole

St Anne's

On the south bank of the River Avon, a little further upstream from the Netham Lock St Anne's Board Mills once stood. At first it occupied nine acres of land, then rapidly expanded to 100 acres. It was built on a historic site, and metal studs had been set in the ground of its car park to mark out the site of the ancient St Anne's Chapel.

The Chapel described by the historian, William Wyrcester as being 19 yards long and 5 yards wide, was founded by one of the Lords de Warr. In the fourteenth century it belonged to Keynsham Abbey who appointed the priests.

The Bristol Guilds of Cordwainers and Weavers kept two enormous candles at the altar, and they remained continually burning for a whole year, being renewed at Whitsuntide.

The Chapel was decorated with votive offerings, including model ships. St Anne was the Patron Saint of sea-faring men and these ships were gifts from sailors and were probably carved during their long sea voyages.

In its heyday the Chapel vied with Walsingham as a place of pilgrimage. It was visited in 1485 by King Henry VII and his Queen, and she returned to the Chapel again in 1502.

At one time, Bristol was proud to own a fleet of pilgrim boats, which brought pilgrims from Bristol up the River Avon to St Anne's Chapel. The boats had names such as – *St Anne of Bristol, St John of Bristol, St Christopher of Bristol*, and *St Catherine of Bristol.*

There was also St Anne's Ferry which for hundreds of years had carried passengers across the river. The ferry was under the jurisdiction of Keynsham Abbey, and in the record of rents in 1540 by the King's Bailiff, mention is made of a certain Thomas Newman who paid 12p for the passage to St Anne's.

For the most part of its long history the ferry continued to function placidly and uneventfully. Pilgrims, workmen and others, used the ferry, paying the toll to the boatman.

In the medieval period there was widespread belief that St

45

Christopher was a ferryman, and so around the ferries a wealth of popular myths emerged. The ferrymen's houses were built alongside the river, and it was said that at all costs a wood fire had to be kept burning in the brazier, in case St Christopher should come that way and wished to warm himself. Another belief was that if a wealthy man granted a ferry to a Manor, or a ferry boat bearing a Saint's name on its bow, then he could be sure of a place in paradise. When a ferry led directly to a Holy Shrine, the boatman was entitled to wear the badge of the Patron Saint.

St Anne's Ferry made headlines in 1891 when a law action caused the ferry to be closed for a period. It was then restored along with three ancient Rights of Way, through St Anne's Wood.

St Anne's Ferry was replaced by a footbridge, which was opened to the public on October 27th, 1957.

The Chapel of St Anthony stood near Blackswarth Road and was believed to have existed until 1824. It was erected to shelter pilgrims who, on approaching the north bank of the River Avon, were prevented from crossing over by the state of the tide, the river being tidal until the eighteenth century.

In St Anne's Wood, not far from the Chapel site, St Anne's Holy Well can be seen. Its water was once very cold and clear and was believed to have had curative powers for eye troubles and scurvy.

After the Dissolution of the Monasteries by King Henry VIII, the Chapel began to fall into decay and the Holy Well became a sheep dip. On June 16th, 1924, the Holy Well was restored and made accessible to the public.

By the middle of the seventeenth century, the site of the Chapel and the nearby mill was taken over by the Brislington Pottery which produced Bristol Delft Ware. A century later, in 1772, John Jenkins was in possession of the premises. He used them as a bakery but was at loggerheads with Bristol's Company of Bakers, by not having served a regular apprenticeship to the trade. The Company presented a Bill of Indictment against him for selling great quantities of bread 25 per cent cheaper than trade, and also tried to cut off his supplies of flour.

Timothy Rodes was a later occupant of the site. He fell on hard times, so set up his own mint to produce counterfeit coins. He was arrested when his apprentice tried to use one of the coins and it was refused. But his guileless assistant insisted that he knew it was a good one for he had seen his master make it.

When St Anne's Board Mills was about to be built in 1913, it was a race against time for Mr W.J. Pountney of the Fishponds pottery who, funded by the British Museum, undertook to excavate the site. He was obviously interested in the pottery remains here, but also the foundations of the Chapel. The most interesting finds were made in a well and former cess-pit; this being the place where devious apprentices and other pottery workers had apparently disposed of their mistakes and breakages where the pottery owner would not find them.

Crew's Hole

A vivid recollection of my childhood was the smell of tar. On coming home from school or from playing outside, my mother always insisted that I disinfect my hands by washing them in coal-tar soap.

In those days roads were surfaced with small stones sprayed with tar which was heated in tanks at the roadside. As children we loved to watch this road surfacing operation which included the services of a steamroller of which we were rather scared. With our fascination for the macabre, we imagined it might run amok and flatten us out but the worst that happened was a clout for getting tar on our clothes.

When whooping cough caught up with us we had to walk to Butler's Tar Works on the banks of the River Avon at Crew's Hole where fumes from the tar-distilling were supposed to be beneficial for chest and lung troubles. Crew's Hole at that time was a hive of industry where men of East Bristol toiled in iron foundries. chemical works and other trades. Some industries here were established as early as the eighteenth century. But of all the industries of the early nineteenth century none attracted more public attention than the production of coal-gas, and none more trouble than tar, its bi-product. For the question arose, what was to be done with this troublesome stuff? At one place they tried burying it, at others it was burned. A comparatively small amount was used by John Macadam who gave Bristol the first tarmacadam roads in the country. Another Scotsman used a derivative for waterproofing gabardine cloth to make raincoats and from him we get the name 'mackintosh'.

47

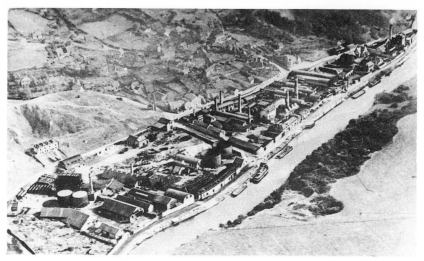

An aerial view of Crew's Hole, early twentieth century.

But the problem of unwanted tar was only solved when it was used in wood preservatives for railway sleepers.

John Roberts and Thomas Daines acquired land at Crew's Hole for a factory to produce creosote and on the recommendation of Brunel employed William Butler to manage it.

The works had been running for about 20 years when, in 1863, fire broke out. A contemporary report described how clouds of smoke could be seen rolling over the city from an easterly direction. The Norwich and Royal Reels set off for the St Philips area and after satisfying themselves that it was not the Alkali Works they reached the Crew's Hole Tar Works, where sheets of flames were leaping high in the air and the heat was so intense that it was almost impossible to get near it.

After this fire, the owners sold the tar works to William Butler. He also leased premises at Silverthorne Lane, from Roberts and Daines, and in the summer of 1879 a telephone was installed so that conversations could be held between both premises. That was eight years before there was a telephone exchange in the city. In 1894, the River Avon overflowed its banks, flooding the works to a depth of four feet and three years later there was another fire. It broke out in the naphtha plant, causing such a blaze as the neighbourhood had never seen before. "Even the river was afire," said the locals.

48

The discovery of aniline dye in 1856 led to further research and established the foundations of the dye industry. This industry needed fine chemicals obtainable only from tar distillers, thus creating a demand for anthracite, naphthaline, benzene and other compounds.

Butler's also extended their trade in other directions as the demand for tar became insatiable.

The Company bought a vessel to fetch tar from the south-west coastal towns, Ireland and France. They also had trows, small river boats used extensively in Wales, which plied across the Severn to South Wales, and returned with coal. The Bristol pub, the 'Llandoger Trow', was named after these boats.

There was also a fleet of barges with names such as *Carbolite*, *Jean*, *Jolly* and *Darby*, which brought tar from Canon's Marsh gas works, and from as far up the river as Bath, Bradford-on-Avon and Reading.

In days gone by it was a great sight to sit on the banks of the River Avon and watch the river craft going up and down the river, sounding their sirens and hooters, communicating in their own special language.

Butler's changed its name to Bristol & West Tar Distillers in 1952 and it then passed to the British Steel Corporation.

The development of Crew's Hole as a residential area has obliterated all traces of Butler's and other industries, which now survive only as photographs.

Butler's barges were also used for works outings. Here, the "Jolly" ferries workers up the River Avon on a Whit-Monday outing in 1912.

Nine

The Cotton Factory

The peace of rural Barton Hill was shattered the day that artisans and navvies moved in. They delved into the earth, then erected a five storey building – this was the Great Western Cotton Factory. It was completed in 1838.

Each morning, as its early morning bell rang out, hundreds of employees living in the surrounding areas, hurried towards the factory. The men were greatly outnumbered by the women and girls, who wore plaid shawls over their heads and shoulders, a fashion set by some Lancashire lassies, who had come to Bristol as key-workers.

On their way to the factory they passed two ancient houses. One had the curious name of 'The Royal Table', and the other was Tilly's Court, better known as 'Queen Anne House'. It is said that the house got its name after Queen Anne paid a short visit here when it was owned by Sir Thomas Day.

At one time the Great Western Cotton Factory was one of the largest textile factories in the country. Its shuttles flew swiftly, producing calico which equalled the quality of that manufactured in Manchester. This calico, and cotton thread, was dispersed all over England and from The Feeder landing stage many consignments were loaded onto ships for export.

A payroll of 1840 showed the factory to be employing over 1,000 workers, many now coming in from places as far away as Kingswood and Hanham. Soon there was a great demand for homes near the factory and Barton Hill, hitherto a quiet almost unknown spot, became a populous parish. Streets of houses were built, but living conditions were deplorable, with no piped water and lack of efficient sanitation.

The earlier streets were named with reference to the Great Western Cotton Factory – Manchester Street, Great Western Street, and Phoenix Street, which took its name from the factory's main mill. Others commemorated some of the early owners such as Aitkin, Maze, Bush, and Pinney. Herapath Street was named after William Herepath, born at the Packhorse Inn Lawrence Hill, who was a Fellow and Lecturer on Chemistry and Toxicology at Bristol Medical School.

As Barton Hill developed and expanded, it became necessary for the inhabitants to have a resident doctor, and in 1846 Dr William Edward Day set up a practice here. Within a few years he was coping with a cholera epidemic, which had started in Bristol and spread to Barton Hill.

The cotton factory proprietors were almost solely responsible for the building of St Luke's Church, and they also provided a school for the children in a large underground room which ran almost the whole length of the building.

In 1859 Archibald Vickers, manager of the cotton factory gave evidence for a commission enquiring into the condition of working people.

He said that the children were 'half-timers', some attended school 9.30 to 12 noon and worked in the factory from 2 to 4 p.m., while others worked in the factory mornings and were at school in the afternoons, the two groups periodically changing shifts.

Mr Vickers also said that there was now a good deal of teetotalism at Barton Hill, and that people read their Bible. He was pleased to add that the daily dinner hour fights at the factory no longer took place, and that parents were anxious for their children to benefit by the education at the factory school.

Then came the Cotton Famine between the years 1861 and 1865, brought about by the lack of raw cotton imported from America during its Civil War. Conditions were bad, and production at the factory was almost brought to a standstill.

These were the years of great deprivation for the local community. In the wake of unemployment came malnutrition and near starvation, the young children, the sick, and the elderly shivered in the unheated homes. Soup kitchens were set up to help the situation, but the death-rate increased.

When adequate imports of raw cotton were once more available things began to improve. Pubs and Christian churches of various denominations were all part of the scene, and adult education classes and recreational clubs were established.

In the 1880s, Marian Pease, the daughter of one of the Cotton Factory proprietors, started the Cotton Girls Club. She brought in yards and yards of unbleached calico for the girls to make petticoats. It was voted 'dreadful stuff' but on the lighter side they had games and music and were encouraged to express their opinions in friendly discussions.

Entrance to the Cotton Factory, Barton Hill, by Samuel Loxton.

The cotton works went on strike in 1912 and with so many women involved, the politician Margaret Bondfield came down from London to try to settle it. Here she found "pitiful groups of unorganised women, working for the miserable pay of eight shillings per week [40p]". The work was hard, and some women had become deaf through years of working with the loud clattering of the looms. "The poverty was terrible," she said.

It would seem that the Cotton Factory was never a pronounced success financially. After the Cotton Famine the original partners pulled out and it was reformed as a limited company, but it was dogged by misfortune until it finally stopped production in 1925.

The following year it was sold to the Western Viscose Silk Company, but this artificial silk venture could not survive the Depression era and it closed in 1929.

The Cotton Factory building remained standing in defiance of Hitler's bombs, but was demolished in 1968.

Ten

Portrait of Mary Robinson – Jacob's Wells – The Seaman's friend

Portrait of Mary Robinson

Mary Darby, the daughter of a wealthy Bristol Merchant, was born in the latter half of the eighteenth century, at Minster House, a building which once stood near Bristol Cathedral. She was educated at Hannah More's expensive school in Park Street, a place which catered for the daughters of Bristol's 'elite'.

On the way to this establishment she walked across College Green where she saw well-dressed ladies and gentlemen strolling leisurely across the grass, and was fascinated by their elegance. Looking down the hill she would have seen the tall-masted ships, their sails furled as they loaded and unloaded their cargoes and if the wind was in a certain direction, there would be a smell of tar and a stench from ships which had carried slaves from Africa to the West Indies.

When she was still a young girl her father had invested unwisely and lost his money in a whale-fishing concern. With no thought for his family, he deserted them and went off with his mistress.

By the time Mary was 16 years of age, she was married off to a solicitor named Robinson, but the marriage was doomed to failure, and Mary was left alone to bring up her young daughter.

The glamour of the theatre, and the adulation received by its actresses and actors, enticed her in to this profession.

As Mary Robinson she became a well-known actress and reached the peak of her success in a play called *Perdita*, in which she played the name part, receiving great applause and adulation.

One of her admirers was George, Prince of Wales, who was then in his eighteenth year. He was enchanted and eagerly sought the aquaintance of the beautiful Mrs Robinson. She was often referred to as 'Perdita' and His Royal Highness in turn received the nickname Prince Florizel, another character from the play.

On condition that she gave up the stage, the Prince installed Mary Robinson in a magnificant establishment, and was said to have written her passionate love-letters, and also settled on her a £20,000 bond. She rode around in a magnificent coach, presented to her by the Prince. It was decorated with silver, with a craftily designed coronet of flowers which incorporated her initials 'M.R.' and appeared to many as a Royal Insignia. Her dresses and jewellery were slavishly copied by duchesses for which costumiers charged high fees, while milliners and others also cashed in on her fame.

Several famous artists of the day painted her portrait, but it was the one by Gainsborough which received the greatest acclaim. Another, by Romney was almost equally well received.

When King George III became aware of the Prince's association he was furious. Although he had no objection to his son taking a mistress, he greatly disapproved of the wealth which had been lavished upon her. The affair ended abruptly. Someone acting for the King got possession of the love-letters and the £20,000 bond leaving Mary with only her coach and an annuity of £500. The romance of Perdita and Prince Florizel was over.

Under the name Tabitha Bramble, Mary Robinson wrote poems, novels and also wrote columns for the *Morning Post*. She visited Paris as a guest of Marie Antoinette. The French Queen admired her beauty and her flair for wearing fashionable clothes and so it seemed that the scene was set for her to become once more 'Society's Darling', but fate had decreed otherwise; on her return to England, she caught a severe chill which left her a chronic invalid and then after an unfortunate affair with a Colonel Tarleton she found herself penniless. She appealed to the Prince for help, but none was forthcoming.

Bristol born Mary Robinson, trend-setter of fashion, successful actress and former Royal mistress died in the year 1800, friendless and impoverished, nursed by her daughter, the one person in her life who had remained loyal.

Gainsborough's portrait of Mary Robinson hangs in The Wallace Collection, London.

Jacob's Wells

Bristol's first theatre was a crude building which stood at Jacob's Wells. It was opened by John Hippisley in 1729, and was popularly known as 'The Hut!'. It had quite a patronage. There were, of course, those who paid to get inside and take a seat, and then there was a far greater audience who assembled on nearby Brandon Hill, in order to see the players in their costumes. This they were well able to do, for the theatre was so narrow that when an actor left the stage, he found himself right outside the playhouse. In order to regain entry on the opposite side of the stage he had to walk around the outside, in full view of the non-paying audience.

One night the theatre was packed to capacity, and an even larger crowd than usual was assembled on the hill. For in an effort to boost the dwindling takings, John Hippisley had widely advertised the personal appearance of Madame Cynthia in all her splendour. But this gorgeous creature kept them all waiting in suspense. They cat-called, stamped and became wildly exasperated as Madame Cynthia failed to make an entry. The other unfortunate entertainers put on their acts but were pelted with everything the onlookers could lay their hands on. "We want Madame Cynthia . . ." the cries arose in crescendo. It was then that the management tried to explain that she had already appeared and was shining down upon them, for according to mythology, Cynthia was . . . the moon. The rioteous uproar which followed led to the closing of the city's first theatre.

It is believed that in the reign of King William II, (1087–1100) Jews arrived in the Bristol area, and settled on the slopes of Brandon Hill. Queen Elizabeth's Hospital was built on the site of an early Jewish cemetery. Springs of water could once be seen flowing down to the foot of the hill, where wells were dug. Through the Hebrew association they became known as Jacob's Wells.

The Jews plied their trade as money-lenders. They flourished and became wealthy, their customers ranked from merchants to Kings. Although they paid taxes, they had no 'rights' as citizens, and lived outside of the town fortifications. It is recorded that a Jew who refused to pay taxes was held in Bristol Castle by King John who ordered his teeth to be pulled out for this offence.

The springs of Jacob's Wells supplied water to St Augustine's Abbey, which later became Bristol Cathedral. After several centuries the wells and springs were built over and their actual sites lost. The Bristol Corporation had baths and washhouses built here. Then quite accidentally, a lost well and spring was discovered in 1987 when builders were converting a shop at the corner of Jacob's Wells Road. As they demolished a wall, they brought to light one of Brandon Hill springs, and a small chamber containing a stone bath. On the lintel at the entrance to the chamber was an inscription, at first thought to be hieroglyphics. These were later identified by a Bristol professor as Hebrew and translated them as "To give one health and long life." According to professional opinion this was a Jewish Mikveh Bath, or Ritual Purification Bath, probably built on the arrival of Jews to this area.

About the same time a local man revealed that he had discovered underground arches and tunnels when he had prised up a pavement slab, outside his house, a few yards from where the bath had been discovered.

A hermitage once stood on Brandon Hill, said to have been built by an Irish Saint during Saxon times who sailed across the Atlantic with companions to find the legendary 'Land of Delights'. . . did he find it? . . . we will never know. But this Saint Brendon was said to have built a Chapel on Brandon Hill.

In the time of King Henry VIII this chapel was abolished, and before long a windmill stood in its place, owned by the astute William Rede, Town Clerk of Bristol who had leased the hill for 60 years at a rent of £1.6.8d.

There is a tradition that housewives have the ancient right to hang out their washing to dry on the Jacob Wells side of the hill.

Times gone by, local people would not walk across Brandon Hill at night. Apart from being mugged or robbed there was the fear of meeting up with the supernatural. One of the ghosts of Brandon Hill was that of Jim Falkner, a drummer in the 35th Regiment Foot, stationed in Bristol in 1771. He deserted his regiment and was sentenced to be shot. He was marched from the Guard House in Wine Street to the east side of Brandon Hill, where a large crowd had gathered. He fell dead, shot by his own comrades. After this, folk swore that they could hear the sound of his drum playing a doleful funeral beat.

So one is comforted to see an angel high up on the top of Cabot Tower, holding a golden ship to guard Brandon Hill.

57

The Seaman's friend

A visit to the docks of our seaport towns conjures up a vision of far-away places and romantic names.

Onlookers, passengers and seafaring men now take for granted the safety load-line, which came into being after much campaigning and pressure on the Government by Samuel Plimsoll.

Samuel Plimsoll was born in a house which overlooked the churchyard of St Mary Redcliffe in 1824. His father Thomas was a Civil Servant, who took his family to live in the Lake District. Samuel received his education at Penrith from Jenny Dalton, the wife of a corset-maker, who was often heard to say, "She moulds the heads, while I mould the bodies."

After having set himself up as a coal merchant Samuel Plimsoll tried to interest the Great Northern Railway in his scheme for the transit of coal, but suffered great frustration in this and became bankrupt. He then joined Newton and Chambers, colliery owners and married the stepdaughter of his employer, Joseph Chambers. As a Liberal, he sat in the House of Commons as Member of Parliament for Derby. In 1870 he took over the ideas of a shipowner James Hall, the true instigator of the 'Plimsoll mark'.

Plimsoll amassed a great deal of evidence concerning shipping scandals, covering defective hulls, equipment and machinery, and the great evil of the day – overloading. He set this down in a book, illustrated with photographs of sailors' widows and orphans. When attending a meeting in Leeds he told his audience about a ship which was manned by boys of 17, because older and more wary sailors would not sail her.

Up until 1871, when a man signed on for a ship, he could be imprisoned if he afterwards refused to sail in her, even if he found her to be unseaworthy. There was one case brought to light by Plimsoll where the owners had refused to have their ship surveyed by Lloyd's. In spite of the fact that she had been placed on the blacklist magistrates gaoled her crew of 20 men who had refused to sail her.

Many unseaworthy ships were deliberately allowed to sail to their doom, the crews being lost without trace, leaving behind destitute families. These were referred to as 'coffin ships' which, along with their cargoes, were heavily insured by their unscrupulous owners,. These owners eagerly awaited the news that their ship had sunk so that they could collect the insurance.

To add to the hazards of the sea, the food shipped aboard for the sailors consumption was already unfit to eat.

When Plimsoll's book was published it shocked the nation. His zealous pursuing of his campaign ran him into trouble, and he had to face a libel suit, but he was applauded by the public and became a national figure.

Bristol, the place of Samuel Plimsoll's birth, was quick to recognise his work, and held a banquet aboard Brunel's steamship the *Great Western* in his honour. He was met at Temple Meads Railway Station by Bristol's leading citizens and as he arrived at Hotwells was cheered by a large crowd. The sumptuous banquet was held in the ship's saloon which was brilliantly lit and decorated with flowers.

When he and his party, which included some rather portly figures, were pulling away from the landing stage in a boat, the fact that the public had become 'overload' conscious was made plain. An old 'salt' standing by the quay, who didn't know Plimsoll from Adam, removed his clay pipe from his mouth and shouted, "I'll tell Plimsoll".

The pressure of public opinion forced the Government to set up a Royal Commission and as a result "The Unseaworthy Ship Act" was passed. But sad to say things went on much the same as before; there was no Authority to see that the Act was adhered to and as a result shipowners were fixing their own load-lines. When Plimsoll watched a ship leaving harbour with her load-line eight inches below the surface of the water, he was confronted with the situation. The Welsh skipper had displayed his contempt for the Act, having painted the load-line on the ship's funnel, and saying that he had not been told where the mark was to be placed.

Samuel Plimsoll's anger knew no bounds as he clashed with the Prime Minister and the Board of Trade. By his persistance the Act was amended in 1890 by a new clause which stated,

The centre of the disc shall be placed at such a level below the deckline as may be approved by The Board of Trade and shall indicate the maximum load-line in salt water, which it shall be lawful to load the ship.

Thus Plimsoll 'the seaman's friend', had won a new deal for the men who sailed the seas.

In grateful recognition of the service he rendered to seamen, a bust of Samuel Plimsoll stands on the bank of the River Avon at Hotwells, and a house in Colston Parade, near St Mary Redcliffe, bears a plaque, showing the Plimsoll Mark, and stating that Samuel Plimsoll was born here.

Eleven

Redcliffe – Redcliffe Shot Tower – The barmaid struck a blow for equality

Redcliffe

The suburb of Redcliffe was independent of Bristol until 1255 and was part of the Manor of Bedminster, held by the Fitzhardings Lords of Berkeley. In the year 1200 Redcliffe was competing with Bristol commercially, and at that time was accessed for Taxation of an amount which was equal to that of Bristol.

In the thirteenth century William, Chaplain of Redcliffe, obtained from Lord Robert de Berkeley a spring of water for his parishioners and the Monks of St John's Hospital at the foot of Redcliffe Hill.

This spring which took rise at Knowle, was conveyed by lead pipes by a somewhat winding course down to Victoria Park, Spring Street, York Road, Bedminster Bridge and up Redcliffe Hill where there was a conduit, which was described in the sixteenth century as "a castellette hard by Redcliffe Church without a gate."

The Redcliffe Caves appear to have been regarded in the past as something of a mystery, the question of whether they were naturally formed or man-made often arose.

This underground network of caves had been forgotten until they were rediscovered in the mid-eighteenth century and used as a dump by businessmen of that time for pottery, glass and ashes from the 'Shot Tower'.

The caves also appear to have been excavated in the fifteenth century for sandstone used in glass-making.

There is a school of thought which believes the caves to run under St Mary's Church and stretch down the other side of the hill. The maze in the roof boss of the Church is said to be a plan of the caves, mazes having great significance in the ancient civilisations.

Redcliffe Shot Tower

William Watts was a Bristol plumber of the eighteenth century, who had a strange dream, possibly brought about by having previously seen molten lead dropping from a burning roof on St Mary Redcliffe Church. In this dream he had seen molten lead being poured through a perforated pan, held over a sheer drop. The resultant droplets or globules hardened as they fell and landed in a tank of water below, which prevented them flattening on impact.

This dream was so vivid that he decided to do something about it. Using lead from the old Roman workings in the Mendips he conducted experiments, and in the first one was said to have used his wife's frying pan. The experiments were successful and in 1782 he took out a patent for an improved method of shot manufacture, "Making small Shot Solid throughout Perfectly globular in Form . . ."

Watts lived opposite St Mary's Church on Redcliffe Hill in a house of the Queen Anne period. He took the roof off this house and built a square tower over it to provide the long drop for the globules. He castellated it in Medieval style so that it would not clash or give offence to the church across the road.

Finally William Watts sold his patent to a local firm for £10,000, which he invested in building a rank of houses at Clifton, set up high on the rocks overlooking Hotwells, and known as Windsor Terrace. These buildings required massive foundations, and the tremendous cost of this left him bankrupt.

The barmaid struck a blow for equality

Once upon a time, husbands used to sell their wives for as little as a pint of beer. It was a right men had claimed since Saxon times, when women were regarded as 'goods and chattels'. Sometimes a halter was placed around their necks and they were led to the nearest market place, where they were sold to the highest bidder. But in the last century a blow was struck for sex equality.

Peter Todd was a shy and diminutive young man, who was brought up in the village of Winterbourne. He moved to Bristol and set up a shoemaker's business in Redcliffe Street, where he became prosperous. He had never been attractive to the ladies, so when Jane Jackson a barmaid from a nearby inn 'set her cap' at him, he was elated. She was described as being sturdily built with dark eyes, and flaming red hair. Had he a little more experience with the opposite sex, the colour of her hair should have warned him of her temperament, but the unsuspecting Peter was flattered by her attentions.

He first made her acquaintance when she came to his shop and ordered a pair of shoes. She followed this up by persuading him that he would be better off with a loving wife to help him in his business. He fell in love with her, and soon they were married.

But within a few weeks, Peter was disillusioned. They had frequent arguments from which she always emerged victorious. Very soon she dominated him so completely that it was she who ran both the household and the business. A while later, they began to live together a little more peacefully . . . until she caught him whispering words of love to a female customer.

Jane flew into a rage and went for Peter, knocking him down. She then snatched the scarf from the woman's shoulders and tied it around her husband's neck. Jane dragged her husband out of the shop and led him to the St Thomas Market close by. The neighbours and the young woman followed closely, in lively procession. They were astonished when she shouted, "What offers? He has a nice little business and a house worth £200."

The young woman who had been the cause of the trouble suddenly piped up, "I'll give 'ee eighteen pence for 'im."

At this offer, Peter turned sulky and attempted to pull away but Jane kept a firm hold on him.

A 60-year-old widow enquired if he had any children, and Jane answered, "No, you need not be afraid of that, no one has any claim on him."

The widow promptly offered two shillings (10p).

Jane placed the ends of the scarf into the hands of the widow and accepted the money. The bulky widow having secured her bargain pushed Peter through the crowd.

The next morning the widow and Peter returned to his house to claim his furniture and the tools of his trade. The widow banged hard on the door and Jane opened a window wide throwing out Peter's lasts, awls and stool. These the widow quickly grabbed then made off.

Peter then gently knocked at the door, it flew open and Jane appeared menacingly with clenched fists. Having previously felt the weight of these, and wishing to bear them no further, Peter ran off and was heard to say that any future attachment would be with one his own size.

Twelve

Old Bedminster Characters

The coming of industrialisation quickly robbed Bedminster of its rural charm making it difficult to associate it with the corn mill which gave Windmill Hill its name and Mill Lane, where the watermill ground corn for St Catherine's Pilgrim Hospital. This building stood in East Street where its crumbling remains were swept away with the erection of Wills factory.

Just over 100 years ago, country people fetched their water from a public well known as Luckwell, situated at the junction of Luckwell

Road and Smyth Road. According to legend the name originated with the Civil War, when Cromwell's troops arrived here travel-worn and thirsty. They were said to have filled their helmets with cool clear spring water from the well, and drinking it toasted each other saying "Here's luck". The real origin of the well is lost, but it was always regarded as a lucky well.

Brightbow cottages once stood at the Bristol end of East Street and sheltered some notable characters. Old Mother Pearce, whose cottage was next to the Police Station, cheekily took in 'shady individuals', giving them a night's lodging for which she charged three pence. Next door to her lived an Italian locally known as 'Johnny Icecream', who claimed to be the first man to sell ice-cream at Weston-super-Mare. When he toured the Bedminster streets the kiddies listened for the sound of his concertina, which he played to announce his arrival.

The house on the other side of Johnny was occupied by George Harris and his wife. He was a rag-and-bone man whose cart was drawn by a dog. It was a house of many aromas, for while George filled the back of the house with junk, in the front of their abode his wife sold faggots, peas, pickled onions and cups of boiled rice flavoured with sultanas.

In later days, the trade in Bedminster Parade cockle-shop slowed down when Welsh women from across the River Severn made occasional visits wearing their Welsh plaid shawls and balancing tubs of cockles on their heads, calling out something which sounded like "Cockles a dwelly."

Colourful characters in old Bedminster were in abundance, such as 'Paper Salley' a newspaper vendor who braved all weathers to sell her papers on the street.

Times gone by, Bedminster was known as 'Bristol's Gretna Green'. A man who styled himself as The Reverend Emanuel Collins kept a public house named "The Duke of Marlborough". He supplemented his takings and gained notoriety by charging a substantial fee for conducting irregular marriages. It was rumoured that several high ranking personages availed themselves of this service.

Then there was Professor Stephens, who followed the same profession as the infamous Sweeny Todd, and so was nicknamed 'The Demon Barber'. Stephens attempted to go over Niagara Falls in a barrel but the stunt failed and he didn't survive the fall.

Another old Bedminster character who lived near The Rope

Walk, was Billy the Tinker. He was the subject of much attention due to the fact that he viewed coat buttons with disdain and adorned his coat instead with 'lion' silver shillings. Billy was something of a connoisseur when it came to the business of eating snails. They were his favourite dish and cost nothing, except the trouble to seek out the rare ones which suited his palate. A man from a lodging house near Old Market Street who eyed Billy's buttons with avarice, offered to show him where the choicest snails could be found, then led him to a wood near Bishopsworth. As Billy poked the snails out of the wall with his stick, he was struck on the head with a piece of iron and the man tore the silver shillings from his coat as he lay dying.

The murderer was apprehended when he tried to spend some of the shillings and consequently was sentenced to hang. But he saved the hangman a job, by hanging himself with his own braces.

It was said that Joe Wring was the strongest man in the South Liberty Lane Colliery, and that he was the only man who dared leave his tools at the bottom of the lift shaft, without fear of getting them 'nicked'. It seems that there was a wager as to whether or not he could lift up a 14 stone man on his shovel. He did! and won the bet.

At the end of the shift, the miners would often play cards and gamble in the fields of Ashton. The police on many occasions lay in wait for them to break up the 'gambling dens' and could often be seen chasing the men across the fields and giving them a sharp whack with their truncheons.

As the population of Bedminster increased, so did the number of pubs and places of worship. This gave credence to the saying
"The women of Bedminster prayed more, and the men drank more, than anywhere else in Bristol."

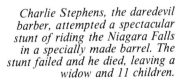

Charlie Stephens, the daredevil barber, attempted a spectacular stunt of riding the Niagara Falls in a specially made barrel. The stunt failed and he died, leaving a widow and 11 children.

65

Thirteen

Kingsdown – The Hotwells Medicinal Spring

Kingsdown

The populating of Bristol's first suburb began in earnest about 1760 when, in order to escape the smoke and grime of the town, Bristol merchants had their new homes built on Kingsdown. This new building development was possibly started by Giles Greville, a prosperous apothecary who purchased an estate known as "The Montagues". In 1737 he divided up the land into plots and to encourage building he provided a popular amenity, the Montague Tavern.

The tavern was later succeeded by the Montague Hotel which became a coaching house on the Old Gloucester Road. It was famous for its turtle soup, reported to have been prepared from an original recipe concocted by a Mayor of Bristol who lived in the thirteenth century. Civic banquets were once held at the Montague Hotel, and it was here that the Colston Boys were taken for their annual ceremonial dram of 'grog'.

Gas-lighting came to Kingsdown as early as 1825 but in 1850 sewerage was still running down Montague Hill in an open gutter.

The quiet country fields near the Montague Hotel were once a favourite spot for duels at dawn. Affairs of honour were still being settled on Kingsdown in the eighteenth and nineteenth centuries. Here, an attorney and man of good standing, Henry Smith, fought a duel with a tailor of Clare Street. Although the tailor was only slightly wounded the injury proved fatal, and on hearing of this, Mr Smith boarded the next ship bound for Portugal.

Many American visitors to Bristol, especially Methodists, make a point of visiting Portland Street Chapel, where its chief founder Thomas Webb was interred. He was Captain of the 48th Regiment Foot, who lost his right eye at the Seige of Louisbourg in 1758, and in the following years played a big part in establishing Methodism in America.

It is said that John Wesley preached his last sermon in the open air at Kingsdown in Carolina Row, 1790.

Perhaps the most interesting story concerning Kingsdown is that of Dame Pugsley's Well or The Virgin's Well.

In 1645 Kingsdown held a strategic position during the Civil War, when its fort on Prior's Hill was staunchly defended and held by Prince Rupert for the King.

At this time a young man named Pugsley who held a commission under Prince Rupert, owned a field on the hill. When General Fairfax, acting under Cromwell's orders, stormed Prior's Hill, Pugsley was hit on the forehead by a stray shot and fell dead on his own land, at a place which was to become Hillgrove Street. After the Royalists surrender to Cromwell's Roundheads, Pugsley was buried with full military honours on the spot where he had died. He left a young widow whom he was said to have married on the same day as he was killed and such a short period of marriage left her a virgin. She vowed to remain faithful to his memory for the rest of her life, and went daily to his grave. It was here that two springs of water issued from the turf and one flowed into a well. This became known as 'Mother Pugsley's Well' and was famed for its curative powers. In the course of time the water became muddy and unusable.

Widow Pugsley died somewhere between the years 1700 and 1705. Accounts of her funeral differ, but one story tells how, according to her wishes, her wedding dress was used as her shroud, and she was carried on an open bier. Her cortège was led by young girls who strew the way with flowers while musicians played merry tunes. She wanted it this way for this was to be her happiest day, when she joined her husband. No muted funeral bell tolled for her, but St Nicholas belfry sounded out a joyful peal of wedding bells.

The Hotwells Medicinal Spring

In 1723 London newspapers were advertising
"Famous Bristol Hotwell Water, fresh from the well, delivered to any part of the Town for six shillings per dozen bottles."

About this time there were no fewer than 15 glass houses in Bristol which no doubt provided bottles for this spa water.

There were several springs in the Hotwells vicinity, but the most important one gushed out of St Vincent's Rock almost under the span of the Suspension Bridge. Its temperature was 76 degrees, and when the river ebbed, it poured out ten feet above the level of the water at a rate of 60 gallons per minute.

The spring was mentioned as early as the fifteenth century by a Bristol topographer and according to Bristol's records Queen Catharine, the much neglected wife of King Charles II visited the spring in 1677.

A strange phenomenon occurred on November 1st, 1755 when the spring water turned as red as blood and became so turbid that it was unfit to drink. Many explanations were put forward but later news reached Bristol of an earthquake which had taken place in Lisbon. So it became accepted that the spa water "had been influenced to an unusual degree by the subterranean fire of the Earth, and had an evident sympathy with volcanic agencies."

The Hotwell House was built in 1696 on a ledge which jutted out into the River Avon. It became a centre of activity, with pumprooms, baths, shops and assembly rooms. This building was the subject of a colour sketch by J.M.W. Turner.

During the eighteenth century the spa became a fashionable resort and was visited by many famous people. The crowds who frequented it played cards, listened to music and exchanged the gossip of the day, while the more energetic paraded along the banks of the river. "To drink the waters" was the excuse used by many in order to enable themselves 'to see and be seen'.

After 1785, Hotwells imitated the City of Bath by appointing a Master of Ceremonies, a Mr William Pennington who wore a gold medallion on a blue ribbon to emphasize the dignity of his office. Elaborate balls were held in the evenings, and public breakfasts in the mornings, as was fashionable in those days.

Towards the end of the eighteenth century, the spa declined rapidly. Large sums of money were spent to prevent the spring being fouled by the river water, but in spite of precautions the spring water became infected and there was a rising deathrate among invalids who frequented it.

The Hotwell House was demolished in 1822 and the ground on which it had stood was removed to make river navigation safer.

The spring was lost for a time and after many complaints in the local press it was piped and enclosed in a grotto hollowed out of the rock. A pump was set up and used until 1913, but by this time the pollution could no longer be tolerated and the entrance was blocked.

All that is left of this once famous spa is a section of the colonnade which stands on the Portway.

Fourteen

Clifton's Royal Resident – Over the Bridge – The Battle of Boyce's Buildings – The Charvolant

Clifton's Royal Resident

Over the years Bristol's Royal York Crescent has attracted quite a number of prominent residents, perhaps none more famed than Eugenie Montijo, who lived at what is now Eugenie House. This was once a finishing school for young ladies, where Eugenie and her sister Paca, daughters of a Spanish nobleman The Duke of Teba, arrived in 1837.

Eugenie came in for quite a bit of teasing and was nicknamed 'Carrots' on account of her red hair, inherited from Scottish ancestors.

At this school there was also an Indian princess who fired Eugenie's imagination with stories of the East and its splendour. Having both come from colourful countries, the pair grew tired and discontented with dull English skies and made a plan to leave England. But Eugenie's sister was cautious and refused to go with them. During a school walk, Eugenie and the Indian princess managed to slip away unseen and made their way to the Bristol Harbour. Here they checked up on the sailing ships to see which were due to leave port. Soon they found an India-bound vessel and without anyone stopping them they boarded her and sat on the deck. But before she set sail, their schoolmistress arrived and took them back, in tears, to Royal York Crescent.

Shortly afterwards, Eugenie and her sister were taken to Paris to finish their education.

Their mother's receptions at Madrid were noted for their elite visitors, one of these being The Duke of Alba, a shy young man with whom Eugenie fell in love. But her mother engineered matters so that he married her favourite daughter Paca. Later Eugenie met Louis Napoleon, the nephew of Napoleon Bonaparte, who at this time was preparing for his transition from President of France to

69

Emperor. On the eve of his coup d'etat Eugenie wrote him a letter of congratulation and as a result both her and her mother were invited to a number of his receptions.

Later, while hunting in the Forest of Fontainebleau, Louis Napoleon proposed to her; they were married in 1853 and Eugenie became Empress of France.

After a visit to England, she was hostess to Queen Victoria and Prince Albert on their return visit to France and when Eugenie's son was born the Queen telegraphed her congratulations within the hour. When the Franco-Prussian War brought about the abdication of the Emperor, Empress Eugenie and her son left Paris and came to England, taking up residence at Camden House, Chislehurst. Here they were visited by Queen Victoria who described it as 'a small house'. It did in fact have 20 rooms, apart from kitchens. Eugenie's friendship with Queen Victoria was one of the great solaces of her life.

Eugenie's greatest sorrow was the death of her son who was known as 'The Prince Imperial'. As an officer in the British Army, he was killed while fighting in the Zulu War.

The exiled Empress Eugenie lived in England until well into the twentieth century. She died in 1920 at the age of 94.

She had seen the start of a new era, when the first pioneers crossed the Atlantic in frail flying machines, such a far cry from the days when she had seen the tall-masted ships anchored in Bristol Harbour.

Over the Bridge

In a programme commemorating the laying of the Clifton Suspension Bridge foundation stone, Mrs Mary Griffiths of Stone Hill, Hanham, broadcast from the B.B.C. West Regional station on August 27th, 1936. She told thousands of listeners how she had achieved the distinction of being the first person to cross the Bridge at its opening on December 8th, 1864.

Mrs Griffiths was 21 years of age at the time and in spite of being considered rather delicate she won an exciting race against a young man who was out for the same honour.

Crowds of people had gathered at the Bridge; there was lots of bunting and flags flying and a large marquee to accommodate special guests and Civic dignitaries. She had managed to get a 'front place' near the Lords Lieutenants of Gloucestershire and Somerset as they performed the opening ceremony.

"Directly the gates were opened," she said, "I ran to the Bridge and started to cross. Then I noticed a man on the opposite pavement running to catch me up. I picked up my skirts and ran faster. I reached the Leigh Woods side a few moments in front of the young man."

Mrs Mary Griffiths died at the age of 94, only a few months after her broadcast.

It's strange how the Clifton Suspension Bridge has a fascination for those in a depressed state of mind – some putting an end to their lives by jumping off it.

There was Sarah Ann Henley who threw herself off the Bridge in 1885. Sarah was 22 years old and was devastated after being 'crossed in love'.

For in her day, being unmarried at this age was considered to be 'left on the shelf.' But her suicide attempt failed. There seems to have been quite a breeze which puffed out her crinoline dress, causing it to act as a parachute and she floated down to the river bank and was rescued un-injured.

Sarah Ann Henley is one of only a handful of people who have fallen from the Clifton Suspension Bridge and lived to tell the tale.

71

It was just after midnight on September 18th, 1896 when Charles Brown took his two daughters Ruby and Elsie on to the Clifton Suspension Bridge. It was a miserable night, cold and raining. As he paid the toll fees, the toll-keeper little realised that he was on a death-mission.

Charles Brown was a Birmingham grocer who was facing bankruptcy, and had come on to the Bridge with the intention of throwing the girls over the parapet, and possibly himself as well.

It was fortunate that just below the Bridge there was a pilot boat riding the high tide. The crew were quick to grab the girls and haul them into the boat. The person principally involved in their rescue was Mr James Hazell, a Pill pilot. The boat pulled in at a nearby landing stage, to get medical help for the girls, who at that point seemed barely alive.

Two policemen were quickly on the scene, P.C. Wise and Sgt Willie; picking up the unconscious girls, they ran all the way to Bristol Royal Infirmary.

Elsie was found to have slight leg injuries and her sister Ruby had spinal injuries but after a couple of weeks was able to get around.

Their father was apprehended and brought to trial. Ruby, the elder daughter was called to give evidence.

"We stayed on the bridge about an hour, I was soaking wet and so was Elsie. Father caught hold of me and I began to scream. He lifted me up on the side of the bridge and put me over."

Charles Brown was found to be insane and was placed in an asylum, relieving him of his financial worries.

Elsie and Ruby Brown were lucky to survive after being thrown over the Suspension Bridge by their bankrupt father. They were rescued by James Hazell.

The Battle of Boyce's Buildings

Thomas Boyce's venture into real-estate was short lived. In 1772 at a cost of £8000, he erected three large elegant lodging houses for visitors to Clifton Spa which became known as 'Boyce's Buildings'. He also built three summer houses, stabling for 34 horses, and a pleasure garden. It was intended that this complex should be a money-spinner, but within the same year he became bankrupt.

Eventually this freehold estate was inherited by William Mathias, but with it came trouble in the form of lawsuits and wrangling which lasted until the end of his life. It concerned an alleged right of way over his property for horses and carriages. Mr Mathias freely admitted to the existence of a footpath connecting Victoria Square with Rodney Place and at the Victoria Square end he built an arch, erected a boundary wall and placed an iron gate there, through which persons could pass on foot. But the Town Council and influential residents of the Square wanted the footpath to become a carriageway. Mr Mathias refused to allow this.

In 1849, a Mr Reed was responsible for removing the boundary wall, and was sued by Mr Mathias. This boundary was frequently knocked down only to be rebuilt again at Mathias' expense. There was great public sympathy for William Mathias but it was obvious that those in authority intended to have their way, and to force a carriageway through his property.

There was the occasion when The Clifton Gas Light Company placed pipes in the ground at Boyce's Buildings; no doubt they had been given permission by 'someone', but certainly not Mathias. There were repeated encroachments on his property, the work often being done at night, in order to conceal the identity of the trespassers and a number of ruses perpetrated for the purpose of establishing a 'right of way' for vehicles.

In 1852, the mail boy with his horse and cart was ordered to pass through Boyce's Buildings on his rounds so as to create a precedence. As a result Mathias had a pit dug across the entrance at Victoria Square, taking care to have it conveniently fenced for the safety of pedestrians. These 'fortifications' earned him the nickname General Mathias, and it was with tactics and obstinacy that he conducted his 'war'.

Of all the charges brought against Mathias, there was one of particular interest. It appears that a lady, Mrs Elizabeth Mais, was walking along the footpath pushing a perambulator when, it was said, Mathias pushed her shoulder and ordered her to go back. But she lifted up the pram with the baby in it and passed through into Victoria Square. A charge for assault was subsequently brought by Mrs Elizabeth Mais which many thought was instigated by the Corporation in yet another attempt to establish a right of way for carriages.

In court, Mrs Mais said that Mr Mathias had not hurt her when he put his hand on her shoulder. The chief witness for the prosecution, a surveyor, admitted that when he had made a survey of the city 37 years previously there was a gate across the pathway, and that no carriage could have passed there without being lifted over.

Those were the days when the fashion for wearing crinoline dresses was at its height, with the skirts having swollen to an enormous size. A little humour was introduced into Court when Mr Mathias' Council asked if a lady whose dress spread the entire width of the pathway, was to be turned back because of a perambulator. Whereupon, Mr Justice Byles thought that the baby's carriage would not be half so formidable an obstruction as the meeting of one lady with another.

The Jury was discharged after being unable to come to an agreement, and the case was set down for trial at the Bristol Assizes in August 1862. This was avoided by private agreement.

For several years afterwards, Mr Mathias found his name before the public concerning his conflict with the Authorities. But eventually they won when William Mathias was sent to prison for Contempt of Court, having disobeyed an order to restore a roadway. At the time he was 92 years old and served six months imprisonment. So many years of conflict had reduced him from a person of wealth and affluence to poverty – thus bringing to an end the Battle of Boyce's Buildings.

The Charvolant

During the horse-races on Durdham Down, Clifton in 1828, Bristolians flocked to see demonstrations of a wind-drawn carriage. This was the brain child of Mr George Pocock, the headmaster of a

75

school for sons of gentlemen situated on St Michael's Hill. He gave this carriage the name 'Charvolant' or Flying Carriage, this being a vehicle drawn by kite traction power.

A few years before, he had watched his son being pulled over the Downs on a wheeled plank to which he had attached his kite. This gave the father the idea that a real carriage could be drawn by an enormous kite, and by 1822 plans were drawn up for the first test of the Charvolant.

This trial run took place between Bristol and Marlborough, and was a cartoonist's delight. The carriage pulled by kites was of a rather unusual design and hitched behind it was a platform set on wheels which carried a rather dejected-looking horse to get the Pocock family home again, just in case the wind dropped. There were two kites, one being 20 ft in length and flying at a height of 170 ft. Apparatus fitted under the axle served to wind up or let out the cord. The carriage was guided by a handle similar to that of a child's scooter.

By 1827 the Charvolant had become so popular that a patent was taken out and advertisements appeared in Bristol papers

The kites and car may be seen at the Horse Bazaar, Portland Square. A set of kites for drawing a car for 3–5 persons 5 guineas. Price of a car nearly the same as a pony cart.

Mr Pocock made strong kites covering them with linen, instead of the usual paper, the latter being easily damaged in stormy weather.

This was one problem sorted out but there was another which he never did quite solve. The kite strings sometimes got entangled with chimney-pots, and angry householders with clenched fists were known to have uttered rude words and to have made unseemly gestures. Kite strings were known to have twisted themselves around church steeples, but the branches of trees proved to be the greatest hazard. On one occasion they got caught up in the branches of a tall elm tree. The carriage overturned and disgorged its passengers on to a grassy bank – no injury except perhaps to their dignity. They were possibly consoled when, according to a passenger, a donkey trotted on to the scene and with a mournful look gave "a most compassionate bray".

Very soon George Pocock's family and friends became adept at handling the flying carriage, as they raced around Bristol and sometimes further afield. They went to Ascot Races, where on seeing

76

the performance of the Charvolant, King George IV, gave it his Royal approval.

No one was quite sure who challenged who, but George Pocock and his Charvolant raced with the Duke of Gloucester's coach drawn by four horses. The race started at a Bristol toll-house and ended at the 'World's End', an inn at St George where a crowd of people were waiting. Some said that Mr Pocock won while others said that he kept up with His Royal Highness, whose horses had galloped hard.

George Pocock and his passengers caused much consternation among the toll-gate keepers, who scratched their heads in confusion as they scanned their toll-boards, but found no reference as to what to charge for horse-less carriages. They were instructed as what to charge for carriages drawn by horses, donkeys and mules, even oxen but there was no mention of carriages drawn by kites, so they were forced to let the Charvolant pass through for no charge. George Pocock seems to have 'jumped on the band wagon', for he described his exemption from the toll as a Regal privilege, saying it made him feel "literally like a king."

Rustics on their way home from the public house were often 'rooted to the spot' with amazement at the unexpected appearance of the Charvolant at night. It passed like a shadow in the moonlight with no sight of horse, nor sound of hoof. This was an eerie experience. They had heard tales of headless horsemen driving carriages but never horseless men riding in a carriage moving by its own volition. "It's the Devil's own work," and "we saw summat outside," they said as they staggered back to the inn.

There were those who wishing to detract from Pocock's achievement pointed out that his flying carriage couldn't move an inch without the wind. But undeterred George Pocock retorted, "Ships might be objected to on this principle." He said that their objection was "trifling" and that, "The absence of winds for several days encouraged the exercise of that noble virtue – patience". He also informed them that with the Charvolant, "there is no jolting, for the weight is partly supported by the kites and the car thus glides over the small hollows, into which other carriages sink."

Mr Pocock built other Charvolants and organised a race between them in which the leading carriage got up to the speed of 25 mph. The inventor made a series of adaptions to his kites, with the idea in mind that kite power could work on waterways as well as land. He went to Liverpool and made an experiment to show that kites could be used for drawing a ferryboat across the Mersey. The success of this experiment was recorded by the *Liverpool Mercury*.

On another occasion a yacht was hired, and after replacing the sails with kites, George Pocock with a large party cruised for three weeks in the Bristol Channel off the coasts of Wales and Devon.

Mr Pocock's invention, described in his treatise on Aeroplaustic Art caused great speculation and wonder in its day, but with the coming of the Railway Age causing great excitement, his brainchild was almost forgotten.

More Bristol Books

Redcliffe Press have now published more than 100 books about the city. Here is a selection.

Loxton's Bristol: A city's Edwardian years in black and white by Samuel Loxton £4.95
A selection of Loxton's black and white drawings which are marvellous exercises in nostalgia, not only for buildings which in many cases have since disappeared but for their evocation of a leisurely age before the motor car.

Offbeat Bristol by James Belsey £2.95
A selection of stories that will astonish, amuse, sadden and fascinate everyone who knows and loves the city – and provide a suitably 'offbeat' introduction to visitors.

Twenty Bristol Murders by Veronica Smith £4.99
Real life, historic stories of crimes of passion and greed that shocked and scandalised the city. Some remain unsolved to this day.

Bristol & Co. by Helen Reid £4.95
A history of old established Bristol firms – from butchers to stockbrokers.

Bristol Between the Wars by David Harrison £4.95
Bristol seen through the eyes of those who lived through two decades of change, richly illustrated with contemporary photographs.

Bedminster Boy: A childhood remembered by Leonard Vear £3.95
The story of childhood during the Depression, and the years leading up to the 1939–45 war.

Bristol: Beyond the Bridge by Michael Manson £4.95
The turbulent story of Redcliffe, Temple and St. Thomas from the Middle Ages to today.

Bristol Observed by J.H. Bettey £4.95
Innumerable visitors to Bristol have recorded their reactions to the city from famous observers like Cromwell and J.B. Priestley to the lesser known, such as Elizabethan soldiers and itinerant preachers.

Bristol in the Fifties edited by James Belsey £4.95
Bristol's best writers recall life in Bristol as it was around 40 years ago.

Bristol Suburban by Mike Oakley £4.95
Comprehensive study of the city's railway network, which is now mostly disused, and a brief history of each station and halt.

The Forgotten Front: Bristol at War 1914–1918 by James Belsey £3.50
This book presents a rare picture of the full tragic impact of the Great War on the city.

Images of Bristol by James Belsey & David Harrison £5.95
A selection of Victorian and Edwardian photographs showing life in Bristol in the nineteenth century.

Siren Nights compiled by the Rev. Paul Shipley £3.50
This collection of eye witness accounts shows how Bristolians faced up to the constant threat of death and destruction during the blitzes.

West at War by James Belsey and Helen Reid £5.95
Personal stories of life during the Second World War from Bristol, Bath, Weston-super-Mare, Gloucestershire and Somerset.

These titles are available from booksellers and some newsagents but if you have any problems they are obtainable direct from us at 49 Park Street, Bristol 1. Why not ask for our full catalogue?